I0003235

Business Intelligence with SAP® BI Edge

Wolfgang Niefert

Thank you for purchasing this book from Espresso Tutorials!

Like a cup of espresso coffee, Espresso Tutorials SAP books are concise and effective. We know that your time is valuable and we deliver information in a succinct and straightforward manner. It only takes our readers a short amount of time to consume SAP concepts. Our books are well recognized in the industry for leveraging tutorial-style instruction and videos to show you step by step how to successfully work with SAP.

Check out our YouTube channel to watch our videos at
https://www.youtube.com/user/EspressoTutorials.

If you are interested in SAP Finance and Controlling, join us at
http://www.fico-forum.com/forum2/
to get your SAP questions answered and contribute to discussions.

Related titles from Espresso Tutorials:

▶ Anurag Barua: First Steps in SAP® Crystal Reports
   http://5017.espresso-tutorials.com

▶ Kermit Bravo & Scott Cairncross: SAP® Enterprise Performance Management (EPM) Add-In
   http://5042.espresso-tutorials.com

▶ Gerardo di Giuseppe: First Steps in SAP® Business Warehouse (BW)
   http://5088.espresso-tutorials.com

▶ Jörg Böke: SAP® BI Analysis Office – a Practical Guide
   http://5096.espresso-tutorials.com

▶ Shreekant Shiralkar & Deepak Sawant: SAP® BW Performance Optimization
   http://5102.espresso-tutorials.com

▶ Rob Frye, Joe Darlak, Dr. Bjarne Berg: The SAP® BW to HANA Migration Handbook
   http://5109.espresso-tutorials.com

▶ Dominique Alfermann, Stefan Hartmann, Benedikt Engel: SAP® HANA Advanced Modeling
   http://4110.espresso-tutorials.com

All you can read:

The SAP
eBook Library

http://free.espresso-tutorials.com

▶ Annual online subscription
▶ SAP information at your fingertips
▶ Free 30-day trial

Wolfgang Niefert
Business Intelligence with SAP® BI Edge

ISBN:	978-1-5191-6894-8
Editor:	Alice Adams
Proofreading:	Christine Parizo
Cover Design:	Philip Esch, Martin Munzel
Cover Photo:	Fotolia #60596613 © Maxim_Kazmin
Interior Design:	Johann-Christian Hanke

All rights reserved.

1st Edition 2015, Gleichen

© 2015 by Espresso Tutorials GmbH

URL: *www.espresso–tutorials.com*

All rights reserved. Neither this publication nor any part of it may be copied or reproduced in any form or by any means or translated into another language without the prior consent of Espresso Tutorials GmbH, Zum Gelenberg 11, 37130 Gleichen, Germany.

Espresso Tutorials makes no warranties or representations with respects to the content hereof and specifically disclaims any implied warranties of merchantability or fitness for any particular purpose. Espresso Tutorials assumes no responsibility for any errors that may appear in this publication.

Feedback
We greatly appreciate any kind of feedback you have concerning this book. Please mail us at info@espresso-tutorials.com.

Table of Contents

Preface

Visual data representation is a hot topic in the age of big data. I would like to take a step back and ask (with apologies to the German philosopher Schopenhauer), do visual representation concepts follow sufficient reason? Honestly, has it ever occurred to well-informed SAP consultants why so many reporting-related tools seem to surface and then disappear? I am sure you have come across more than one ingenious SAP demo where you see nice screens for reporting tools, only to realize not too long after that a new tool is already in the works. In this sense, Schopenhauer, who is notorious for his complex but appealing theories about will and representation, has some commonalities with SAP— things are complicated. In this book, I will review the reporting from a higher level and use an investigative style that puts the reader in "discovery mode." This is designed to help cross-functional consultants survive the jungle of tools and utilize core SAP functionality, which is close to the transactional level. Hence, you will not find the traditional walk-through demos in this book but rather a concept that will help you understand the data and create a framework that you can use in your own projects. This small library of skills can be leveraged better than dozens of tools that fail if just one connection is not in order.

The target demographic for this book includes informed cross-functional consultants who need to understand technology beyond the marketing demo.

I will focus on the source of data and its path to the visual representation in a report or dashboard. How can you find the data in SAP? How can you train yourself to create a repetitious concept to analyze transactions in SAP for reporting? With this focus, I will expand the scope to connect with common BI tools and also relate to SAP HANA. I will walk you from SAP ECC transactions to BI tools and transaction codes to Business Object Universes. Finally, I will show you how all of these connect in SAP HANA without losing track of the core concepts. I will also share a BI Consulting method that focuses on a data audit versus solely focusing on BI Edge and the tools currently included with this product.

Personal Dedication

I believe real knowledge can be found beneath the surface where it enables us to form new ideas instead of following the old ones. I dedicate this book to my wife and kids who lead me down new paths every day.

We have added an icon to highlight important information:

Tips
Tips highlight information concerning more details about the subject being described and/or additional background information.

Finally, a note concerning the copyright: all screenshots printed in this book are the copyright of SAP SE. All rights are reserved by SAP SE. Copyright pertains to all SAP images in this publication. For simplification, we will not mention this specifically underneath every screenshot.

1 Introduction to SAP BusinessObjects Business Intelligence (BI), Edge edition

"We have the answer, but the relevant question has not been asked yet." While this sounds a bit funny, it highlights a core element of modern analytics. You have to know what questions to ask before you can select the right data sources and dig into the data to get the answers in the form of information that you need. In SAP BusinessObjects Business Intelligence (BI), Edge edition (BI Edge) terms, this would mean first defining the semantic layer, then configuring the data, and finally utilizing the business layer. These are the elements of the so-called "universe" (more about that later).

Identifying the right questions to ask is an essential part of this book. A good question to start with is: When do you qualify someone's statement as brilliant? Are you doing so because your own sentiments are mirrored, or is it because they are offering a completely new perspective that enlightens you? I hope that you are like me and are drawn to the power of enlightenment that comes with new ideas.

So what does this have to do with SAP BI Edge? For starters, BI is trying to capture information based on the questions that I asked. Is it possible to extract new information from the "universe" of data that can enlighten us even on the questions that I did not ask?

Don't worry, I will not drift off into a metaphysical discussion. However, I do believe there is power that can be unleashed once the problems are identified by asking the right questions and then delivering a process that employs the tools that are part of the SAP BI Edge suite.

In the following sections of this book, I will identify the key problems faced with SAP BI projects. Then, I will explore an accelerated implementation process to leverage the value in SAP BI Edge tools.

In this book, you will learn how to use BI Edge tools and gain an understanding of the key problems that are common to BI projects within the context of SAP ECC implementations.

1.1   BI business placebo and the SAP shadow theme

Modern ERP systems evolved from the idea that a centralized system can manage processes better than disparate "islands of data." However, a centralized approach often comes at a cost for the end user. The reason is that an integrated ERP system can only provide value if all of the departments and users continuously enter and update the data they produce. Users often perceive this requirement as a constraint that limits the freedom and creativity previously found with Excel, for example.

From a C-Level perspective, though, this looks a bit different. The unified infrastructure allows for strategic management of the enterprise where data is effectively summarized, grouped, and analyzed to drive decision-making.

Consequently, the adoption of SAP and related ERP systems is not a question at the C-Level. It is interesting, though, that the problems found at the micro level where users interact with SAP are still very much the same as they were many years ago. The main reason for this is that, at the micro level, the user has to deal with daily uncertainties and needs practical ad hoc tools for support. On the marketing front, this problem is well known, and new products promise to address challenges with self-service BI and similar marketing-style buzzwords.

There is another problem. SAP end users are conditioned to praise SAP, driven by the fear that they will be labeled as incompetent if they do otherwise. This unofficially establishes a *shadow theme*, which means that users officially support and are happy with the system. Unofficially, however, users feel paralyzed by data entry tasks and the inability to get information out of the system for analysis. When users only utilize the tools provided and stop creating their own methods to improve business processes and efficiency, then the shadow theme is at work. It means that the organizational structures are not optimized to leverage the creative input from employees, and consequently, productivity may be sacrificed.

Essentially, the SAP process standardization leverages the integrated flow of information but may not address the day-to-day operative tasks that need to be accomplished by users. The religious embrace of the system leaves users with an inability to deal with the unknown because they are trapped within an integrated standard process. As time goes by, the user base may even unlearn the valuable skill of dealing with the unknown. For example, a user may say "I cannot do x, because SAP cannot do x."

To further dive into this topic, review the theory of *complex responsive processes*.[1] This theory attempts to explain the dynamics, or inclusion-exclusion, used by human agents. The theory states that there is an inherent level of uncertainty within the organizational life of companies. The standards imposed by systems such as SAP ECC, SAP CRM, etc. can inhibit this essential dynamic process and lead to unwanted results. Consequently, the key challenge with modern ERP business solutions and BI projects is to include a process that allows for dynamic change and integrates the requirements that are yet unknown in the form of a flexible process.

1.2   Problems with BI projects

What are the core problems with BI implementations? The project phases to implement BI tools include the traditional phases from requirements definition to implementation and live operation with maintenance. The project plan aligns the budget with the milestones that achieve the business value. So far, this looks good. The reality, however, paints a different picture. Due to massive infrastructure requirements, as well as the very dynamic structure of BI, projects are delayed. Numerous tools and platforms accumulate in a jumble of technologies and tools, which instead of providing a clearer image of the data, does the opposite—creating an additional layer of obscurity.

The BI Project break-even analysis in Figure 1.1 shows the ideal project investment in red and the value of the project in green. Please note that I indicated the maximum value line. This is meant to highlight that only a certain level of value is reached with the BI tools. Due to the problems related to the shadow theme, the value gained from the BI implementation is limited.

---

[1]   Complexity and Group Processes: A radically social understanding of individuals. Brunner-Routledge, London 2003.

User Value / Investment
Maximum Value Traditional BI/BW
BI/BW User Value
Target Break Even
BI/BW Cost
Time
GoLive
Competitive Edge

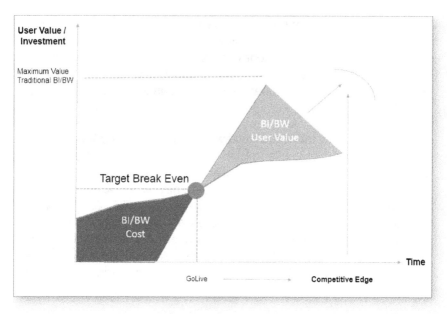

Figure 1.1: BI project break-even analysis

A closer look reveals that the SAP BI Edge suite includes a full set of BI-related tools. The high-level schema graph (see Figure 1.2) shows the BI tools included with BI Edge. Note that the BI tools are independent of SAP ECC.

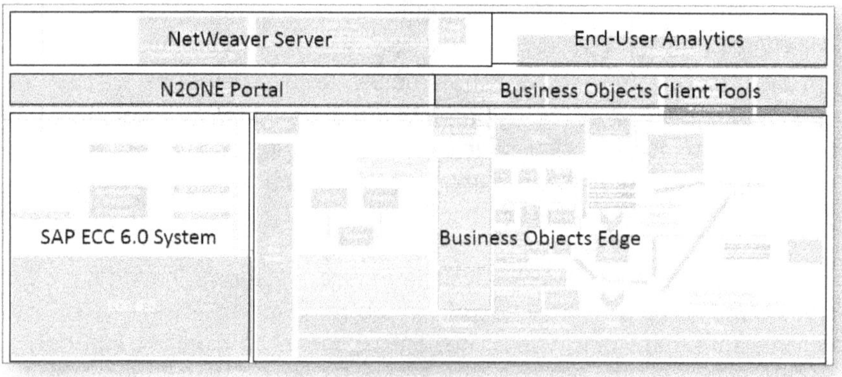

NetWeaver Server
End-User Analytics
N2ONE Portal
Business Objects Client Tools
SAP ECC 6.0 System
Business Objects Edge

Figure 1.2: SAP BI Edge technology schema

The following key problems can therefore be summarized for BI projects:

- ▶ Time to value: BI projects take too long.
- ▶ BI projects have a value maximum.
- ▶ The shadow theme traps knowledge and expertise.

In order to address these issues, I will introduce a method that targets the following aspects:

- ▶ Improve time-to-value with BI.
- ▶ Increase the maximum value of BI.
- ▶ Unleash the potential of the shadow theme and translate it into usable information with reporting apps designed by agile teams.

1.3 The BI consulting method

The BI consulting method I introduce in this book utilizes the tools included with SAP ECC, including SQVI, InfoSets, etc. and aligns their use with a strategic deployment of the BI Edge suite. The priority is to get immediate production use out of each tool while unleashing the trapped potential within the organization and translating it into usable reporting apps.

As shown in Figure 1.3, the BI consulting method begins a BI project by analyzing the SAP module utilization. This will document the current transaction code use across departments and the transactional volume associated with them. With the information collected, I can conclude obvious value potentials that are left unused. For example, I can identify if the features within SAP ECC are utilized or are left unused. In practice, MRP often is not fully configured. The most comment explanation for this is that the implementation team wanted to implement this in a subsequent phase after the go-live. However, then MRP was never implemented.

This information is used as a starting point for BI-related requirements with a focus on identifying the long-term key competitive advantages that the organization wants to achieve and maintain.

The reporting requirements can then be divided into strategic and operative (daily) reports. While the strategic reports are commonly run from within SAP BI/BW, there are a significant number of reports that need to be run on a daily basis. Predominantly, the shadow themed requirements may surface in the form of operative daily reporting requirements.

The strategic reports will be implemented using the BI Edge tools and may use the BW infrastructure where data is summarized, grouped, and ready for analysis. The operative reports may require real-time analysis and may also need to mix and merge with information available outside SAP and within SAP. I will establish agile project groups that are ready to identify those requirements and translate them into reporting apps with immediate results.

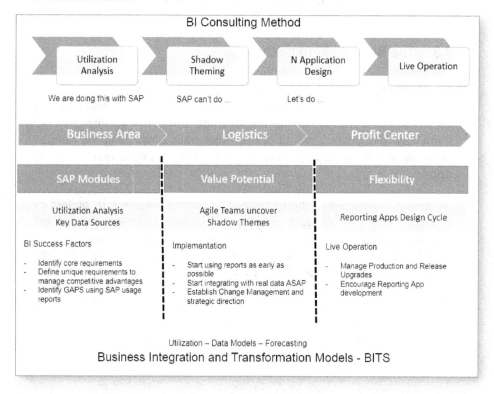

Figure 1.3: Business integration and transformation suite models (BITS)

With this BI project implementation method, I am targeting the established project problems and improving the time to value. I can also raise the maximum value limit because the flexible organization allows it to adapt and integrate new requirements.

Therefore, the BI consulting method achieves a better project break-even point and also increases the maximum BI value (see Figure *1.4*).

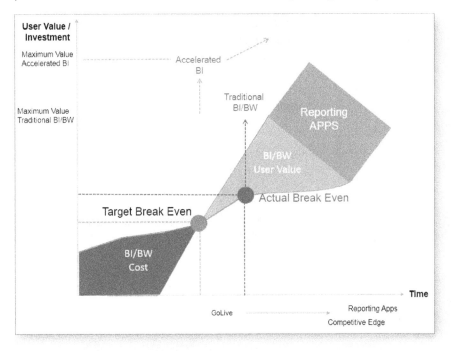

Figure 1.4: *Accelerated BI method ROI improvement*

1.4   Chapters overview

During the course of this book, I will review the available tools that come with SAP BI Edge and position them within the portfolio with regard to the current task, as well as the user skills required. In addition, I will take a critical approach to analyzing the use and implementation of the BI Edge Suite, which differs from the commonly found marketing information you may find on the Internet. The point is that I will add a new and practical angle to using these tools. In summary, the book will shine light on information blurred by marketing information that does nothing more than feed a business placebo with new products and technologies.

In Chapter 2, I will review all of the products and tools available in the BI Edge toolset. This includes the positioning of the most critical products in a diagram. I will also briefly discuss the published roadmap with relevance to the existing product versions and new releases. Furthermore, I will review some important installation and setup tips for BI Edge with SAP ECC.

In Chapter 3, I will introduce a case study. This case study forms the core of the BI consulting method, which I introduced in Chapter 1. In essence, I will establish a practical approach that guarantees fast results and re-solves the delayed break-even point on larger BI projects. In this chapter, I will further position the BI Edge tools and try out them out as part of the case study. I will also define the core elements of a strategic reporting framework.

In Chapter 4, I will explore the query and reporting tools that are built-in to SAP ECC 6.0. These tools form the platform for efficiently using BI Edge tools.

In Chapter 5, I will discuss how to leverage reporting functionality, such as running Crystal Reports using InfoSets created in SAP ECC. I will also explore the limitations of this concept.

In Chapter 6, a universe will be created by expanding upon the knowledge gleaned from the concepts reviewed in previous chapters. You will learn the operative and strategic perspectives for these con-cepts.

Finally, in Chapter 7, I will walk through a sample solution that publishes SAP reporting data in a web-friendly format.

2 Introduction to BI Edge 4.1

In this chapter, I will review the BI Edge Suite tools available from SAP. These tools are updated regularly. That is the primary reason why focusing on tools is not as effective as focusing the process.

2.1 BI Edge products and technologies

The BI Edge suite includes a full set of reporting tools that can be organized by function and complexity. For example, there are end user tools with lower levels of complexity, such as BI Launchpad and Xcelsius. The value of these tools is highly based on the infrastructure available to the project team. This infrastructure is designed with server-based tools that may be more complex, but are primarily designed for use by technical admins. For example, the Universe Design Tool creates the semantic layer and data connections in a hierarchy to publish relevant information in a business layer. The business layer data can then be consumed by BI Launchpad and Xcelsius applications. In the case study, I will configure a full information workflow example. Figure 2.1 highlights that there may be many tools and layers involved in generating a report that is embedded within a corporate reporting strategy. For some, this graphic may also highlight the jumble of tools and interface technologies within the solution architecture.

Figure 2.2 shows a partial view of the technologies and highlights the process from semantic to data and the business layer in red. You need to keep in mind that these three layers are at the core of the BI Edge concept; they are essentially the building blocks of the universe concept. Therefore, if you want to create a report in BI Edge, you very rarely just create a query and use the reporting tool to create a list and/or graphical visualization. The idea is that you can utilize a complex network of data sources, which you would connect on the lowest level called the semantic layer. By *semantic*, I mean the logical language established for reports, which will be represented by the data sources selected for the reporting infrastructure.

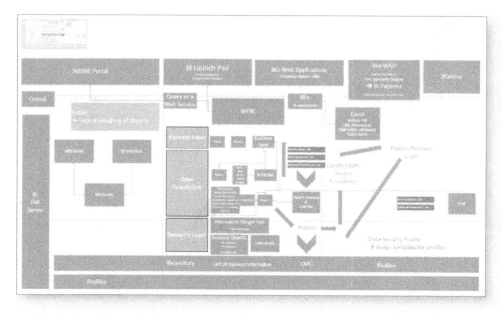

Figure 2.1: BI tools jungle

This selection will define the scope of data to deal with in reports. However, these data sources may have different representations of data and multiple areas of business focus. For example, there could be manufacturing and CRM data from various sources that may have unique column names for data. On the data foundation layer, this data is organized and prepared for business use. Then, in the third layer, the data is logically aligned with a business focus so that it can be easily understood by functional consultants for reporting.

While at first glance this may sound like a lot of overhead, the concept makes sense when you have complex data sources with multiple layers of privileges for user groups and departments. However, you are right that, for a simple report and ad hoc reporting, this concept may be perceived as a headache for a user who just needs to create a quick report in Excel. However, in the long run, the problems you face creating a mess of quick and dirty reports will be resolved with the organizational structure of the layered concept introduced with the universe.

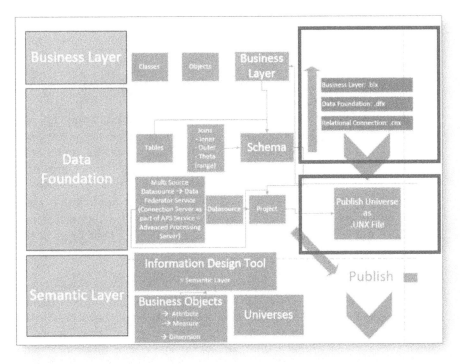

Figure 2.2: BI universe layers

In the following section, we will look at the BI Edge tools. In addition, we will review the tools that are already built in with SAP ECC. You will also learn how to connect them.

2.2 SAP ECC 6.0 reporting

BI Edge tools include the following applications:

- ▶ CMC Licensing
- ▶ Information Designer
- ▶ Universe Designer
- ▶ Crystal Reports

- ▶ WEBI
- ▶ Query as a Service
- ▶ BI LaunchPad
- ▶ Xcelsius

The *CMC – Central Management Console* is designed to manage the administrative overhead not covered by other tools. Essentially, the CMC must be used to manage the license for BI Edge, which will then determine the tools available to users. In BI Edge 4, a certain number of data services are included. However, the full feature set of data services is not included by default. The data services are a separate product that allow you to further integrate various data sources via service connectors and present the information by means of the semantic or data layer in the universe.

The *information designer* is the new version of the universe designer in BI Edge 4.x. It will replace the universe designer in future releases. Please note that, due to compatibility issues, you may have to use the universe designer for some older production systems. However, if you are deploying a new project, you can use the information designer.

One of the core reporting products in BI Edge is *Crystal Reports*. Crystal Reports can connect to data sources directly or also use BI Edge universes.

A *WEBI* is a Web Intelligence document that can be run in a browser. It usually integrates graphical representations of the data which are combined with a grid.

The *Query as a Service* tool is of particular interest, as using this technology efficiently is very powerful. Essentially, you can create a web service based on a query and then consume the web service in Xcelsius. I will look at this functionality further as part of the case study.

Xcelsius is an Excel-based add-on that includes various widgets to present data as a dashboard. For example, you can connect relevant data based on web services and drive graphics.

Figure 2.3 shows the BI Edge tools and also lists the InfoSet as part of the SAP ECC 6.0 built-in tools. As part of an accelerated BI implementation, a core aspect of the reporting strategy includes built-in reporting tools to help drive the BI Edge reports. The InfoSets will also be used during the case study. In fact, the first report created will use the InfoSet concept in SAP ECC 6.0.

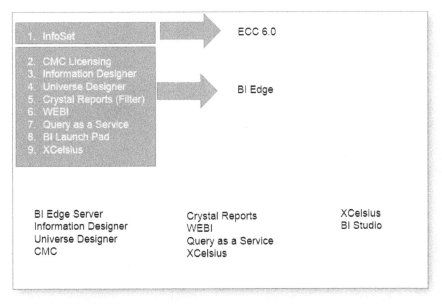

Figure 2.3: BI Edge tools

2.3   SAP BI Edge editions

The license code will determine the specific BI Edge product edition available to you. The license code is noted in the license management section of the CMC (see the details in Figure 2.4).

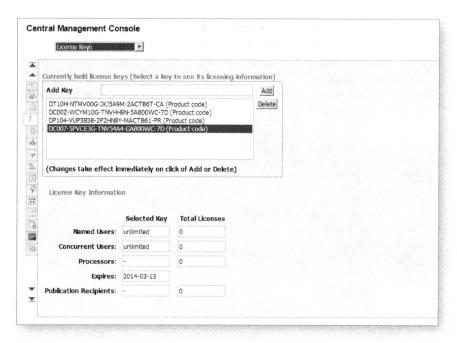

Figure 2.4: CMC license screen

The following BI Edge editions are available. Please note that these packages may change as SAP makes updates.

SAP Business Objects BI, Edge Edition, **Standard Package:**

▶ This package includes the BI platform for scheduling and publishing reports, including the information designer for semantic layer design.

▶ Crystal Reports with semantic layer integration. This lets users design and aggregate data sources using the information design tool in Crystal Reports.

▶ SAP WEBI – Web intelligence.

▶ Advanced Analysis.

▶ Business Objects Explorer.

▶ Dashboard design.

SAP Business Objects BI, Edge Edition **with data integration:**

▶ In addition to the standard package, this version also includes the ETL (Extract Transform and Load) data services. *ETL* is a data services environment that allows the user to automatically collect data from various sources in the form of automated workflow style services.

▶ Impact analysis and data lineage for data services.

SAP Business Objects BI, Edge Edition **with data management:**

▶ This edition adds more data quality management for larger enterprise environments – in particular, the global address cleansing feature. However, this product is not within the scope of book.

2.4 SAP BI Edge installation tips

When you install BI Edge, you will run through the standard installation wizards. However, there are a number of things that you should be aware of. Keep in mind that this information may change as SAP updates its products. Therefore, I have chosen to focus on the core aspects that may apply across versions.

When you install BI Edge, a separate SQL instance is created by default. This instance is called `<Your Server>\BOE140`, as in the example shown in Figure 2.5. This instance holds information about your BI Edge configuration. For example, any adjustments you made using the Central Management Console (CMC) will be saved in this BI Edge Content Management System (CMS).

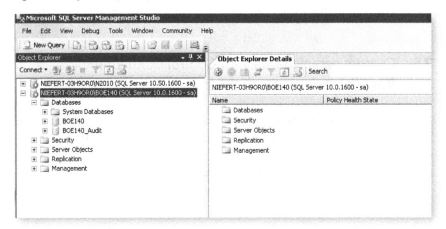

Figure 2.5: SQL instance for BI

When you log on to the BI Edge installation using the CMC), you have a drop-down menu to select the type of authentication. If you do not have a specific enterprise setup, you may want to log in to the installed instance. If the CMS option is not available, you may proceed to create a custom parameter file.

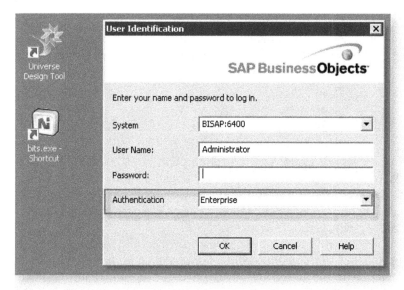

Figure 2.6: Login window

The problem you may encounter is that the drop-down does not offer the CMS option. This problem may occur with various BI Edge tools when trying to log in. In that case, you may also consult the parameter files.

2.5 Custom parameter files for Control Configuration Manager

The CONTROL CONFIGURATION MANAGER as shown in Figure 2.7 displays the critical services related to your BI Edge system installation. If you want to connect to the CMS or run a report publishing function, then you have to make sure these services are running.

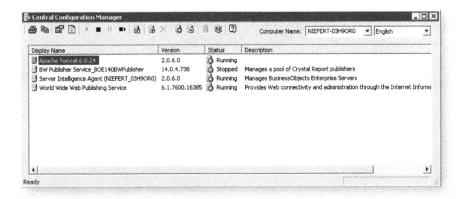

Figure 2.7: Central Configuration Manager

In order to set the defaults for each application, you can consult the parameter files in this directory:

```
C:\Program Files (x86)\SAP BusinessObjects\
Tomcat6\webapps\BOE\WEB-INF\config\default.
```

In order to make a change, create a text file in the directory

```
C:\Program Files (x86)\SAP BusinessObjects\
Tomcat6\webapps\BOE\WEB-INF\config\custom.
```

For example, you could create the file "BIlaunchpad.properties" that can include custom configuration parameters to allow you to connect with the CMS.

```
cms.default=servername:portnumber
cms.visible=true
```

Note that, once you create a parameter file, you need to restart the Apache Tomcat Services.

You can parametrize the user experience for each BI Edge tool using this type of parameter file. This includes custom products names in the login window, etc.

2.6 SAP ECC and BI Edge transport files

If you want to use SAP BI Edge alongside an existing SAP ECC 6.0 system, you need to install the transport files. You can find the transport files in the folder shown in Figure 2.8.

```
/Data_Units/Transports/Unicode_compatible/data
```

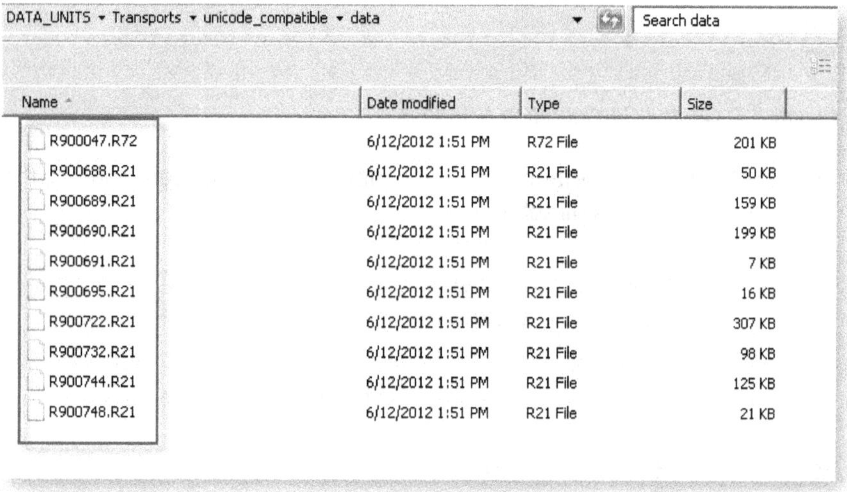

Name ▲	Date modified	Type	Size
R900047.R72	6/12/2012 1:51 PM	R72 File	201 KB
R900688.R21	6/12/2012 1:51 PM	R21 File	50 KB
R900689.R21	6/12/2012 1:51 PM	R21 File	159 KB
R900690.R21	6/12/2012 1:51 PM	R21 File	199 KB
R900691.R21	6/12/2012 1:51 PM	R21 File	7 KB
R900695.R21	6/12/2012 1:51 PM	R21 File	16 KB
R900722.R21	6/12/2012 1:51 PM	R21 File	307 KB
R900732.R21	6/12/2012 1:51 PM	R21 File	98 KB
R900744.R21	6/12/2012 1:51 PM	R21 File	125 KB
R900748.R21	6/12/2012 1:51 PM	R21 File	21 KB

Figure 2.8: Transports

The transport files will install the necessary drivers and files that will allow the SAP ECC system to connect with the SAP BI Edge tools. If you do not install these transports, then you may experience connectivity issues or other related problems.

The transport installation in the SAP ECC system is done using the transaction code STMS (see Figure 2.9).

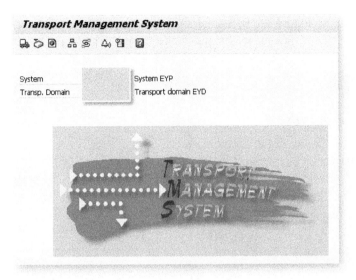

Figure 2.9: SAP Transport Management System

You can consult the file `transports_EN.txt`, which explains which type you must install: ANSI or Unicode. The ANSI version is for SAP Basis systems earlier than 6.20. The Unicode version is for SAP Basis 6.20 and later. You then copy the folder cofiles in `usr\sap\trans\cofiles` and data in `usr\sap\trans\data`. To import the transport, you must use the STMS transaction (see Figure 2.10).

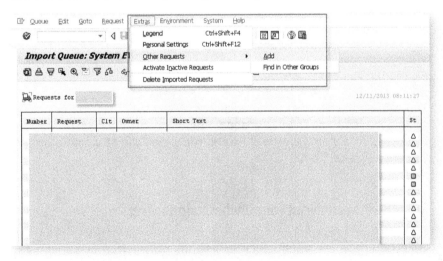

Figure 2.10: Transport status

From the menu in Figure 2.10, select OVERVIEW and then IMPORTS. Double-click on QUEUE. Then, in the top menu, select EXTRAS • OTHER REQUEST • ADD. From the drop-down menu, select the request. Now you will find the request in the queue. Repeat for all transports as necessary (see Figure 2.11).

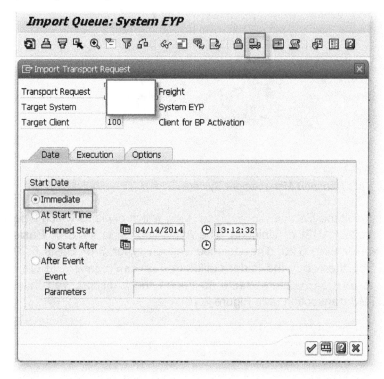

Figure 2.11: Transport scheduling

You can run the transports immediately to make sure that your SAP ECC system is prepared. These transport integration steps are commonly ran by your SAP admin. However, I want to mention the steps here so that you are aware of them.

2.7 SAP system not found when connecting

Once you have the parameter files and the transport in place, you can still run into a situation where you want to select and connect to an existing SAP system. Some BI Edge tools use the SAPLogon.ini file. You may have to adjust the environment variable and modify the saplogin.ini file on your system where the BI Edge tools are running.

You can also create the environment variable SAPLOGIN_INI_FILE. This environment variable points to the .ini file, which is commonly placed in the following path (see Figure 2.12):

```
C:\Users\Administrator\AppData\Roaming\SAP\Common\
saplogon.ini
```

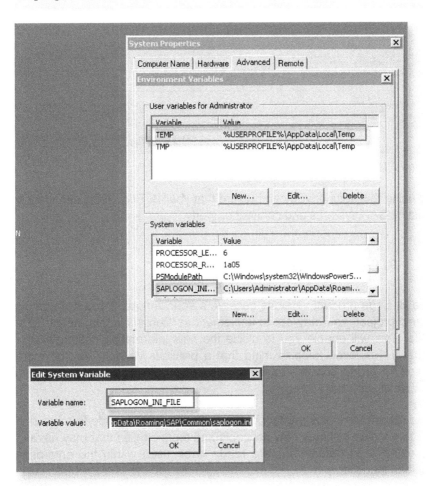

Figure 2.12: Variables to review

Make sure the saplogon.ini file is saved in UTF-8 format (see Figure 2.13).

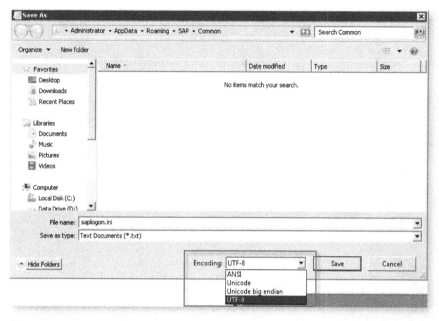

Figure 2.13: Update saplogin.ini

By using this setting, you can be sure that your BI Edge tools can identify existing SAP systems and connect properly.

2.8   BI Edge product history

The BI Edge product versions deserve a special note. If you are starting a new project, you may opt to implement version 4.x within the BI Edge suite. This will enable you to utilize the new information designer functionality. However, keep in mind that a previous version may be more suited for production use based on the overall requirements and system complexity you have to cover.

One reason for this is the fact that a major release upgrade from version 3.x to 4.x also includes new concepts and technologies that may have to be established before they are ready to be used within the enterprise solution landscape.

2.9   BI Edge positioning of included applications

You can picture the BI Edge tools in a graph based on the analytical skills required and the level of end-user friendliness. While this portfolio seems complete, it also uncovers a big gap for end user tools. The most common platform for end-user analytics and reporting today is Excel. However, Excel is basically not covered, or only indirectly covered, using the available tools. I am sure many SAP enthusiasts will disagree and claim that there are many ways to leverage Excel. However, none of the available options can stand its on their own, as Excel requires some other infrastructure to be in place to be usable.

We will revisit the chart in Figure 2.14 a few times during the course of this book with additional information.

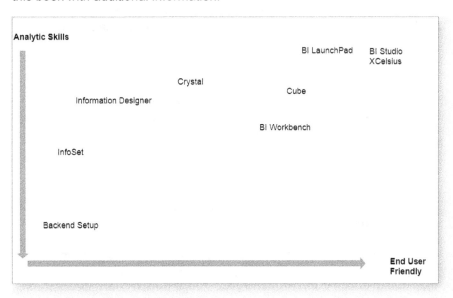

Figure 2.14: Positioning the tools

2.10   BI Edge roadmap

The relevance of any roadmap for SAP products must be considered with SAP HANA in mind. I am suggesting this because SAP HANA may be the most groundbreaking SAP platform since the introduction of R/3. Therefore, you can expect that many of the tools discussed in this book will eventually somehow be integrated or replaced by SAP HANA tools and data services.

The BI Edge technologies will evolve into the open Eclipse platform and be merged with the SAP HANA (Design) Studio.

You can find details about BI Edge products on the official roadmap page: http://service.sap.com/roadmap.

2.11 Types of reports within the enterprise

Before I move any further with reporting tools, let me quickly clarify the types of reports commonly looked at in an enterprise. The reports can largely be organized into strategic reports, which will often be covered by BW; ad hoc reports; and operational reports, which need to be run by users without further consulting BW.

Reporting types include:

- ▶ Strategic reports: BW, cubes, analysis.
- ▶ Operational reports: Real-time information.
- ▶ Ad hoc reports: User interactive reports.

The main characteristic of strategic BW reporting is that the data is extracted using predefined extractors to organize relevant data for analysis. However, this means that the data is often not real time because it must be synced from the ERP system with BW.

An example of a typical BW report is a sales analysis report with a year-to-year comparison. Here, data is collected and grouped in BW prior to running the report. Examples of operational reports are: sales orders in the past hour, web orders placed within the last two hours, and shipments made within the last hour.

With the information provided thus far, you may conclude that the strategic reports are mostly the ones that utilize BW and require that the information be treated and massaged accordingly to be ready for analysis by subject matter experts.

The operational reports may require more direct access to data to shorten the journey from data source to analysis. Therefore, BW may not necessarily be consulted as a data source but rather connect with the SAP ECC system directly. It depends on how much delay you can afford when evaluating the value of the information presented.

In addition, there is a set of requirements that are not part of the defined requirements. These are the day-to-day requirements that need to be covered. The users need new reports quickly and every day to analyze. In order to avoid feeding into the shadow theme, a strategy is needed to address these. In particular, I will utilize the BI consulting method introduced in Chapter 1 in the case study to arm users with the necessary tools to achieve their ongoing reporting requirements.

Finally, it is important to note that more data and better analytics does not equal better information. It is important to define a BI strategy that ensures that you ask the right questions.

2.12 Enterprise perspective versus end user problems

BI Edge products can effectively cover your reporting and analytical reporting needs. However, I want to ensure that the end user perspective is not neglected in this book. In particular, how the BI Edge tools can help the common SAP user resolve their daily reporting needs must be determined, without having to undergo a large reporting and BI project to establish the relevant infrastructure. As mentioned previously, this is largely an organizational aspect. During the initial scoping of the BI project, it must be ensured that a platform is established that allows users to define and implement their reporting requirements on a daily basis. Those reporting solutions will evolve as reporting mini-apps, which will then be used as part of the ongoing refinements to optimize the enterprise reporting architecture. For example, a new departmental report that was created as part of a reporting mini-app will be used as a requirement to define new universe structures that can then be leveraged across the enterprise outside the limits of the department where the reporting mini-app was designed.

3 The BI case study and the top two SAP transaction codes

In this chapter, I will introduce the tools needed by power users to translate their requirements into manageable mini-reporting apps. In order to gain a solid understanding of this process, I will share a detailed case study.

The case study in this book has two components. The first part focuses on the BI consulting method and the idea that system utilization is an indicator for how users navigate and accomplish their tasks. It forms the basis to identify utilization exceptions, which surface either in the form of unused features and/or missing features.

I will review basic auditing methods to obtain this information. Once this is done, I will continue in Chapter 4 to create actual reports for the ecommerce example, which forms the second component of the case study.

First, I will walk through the tools you need to structure reporting requirements for your SAP system using the concept of system utilization analysis.

You can then follow the same steps when it comes to your own requirements. During the course of the case study, I will also introduce the most two most important transaction codes in SAP. You may wonder—what are the most critical transaction codes in SAP? I'll share more about the top two candidates later in this chapter.

3.1   SAP BI consulting method and system auditing

The BI consulting method discussed in Section 1.3 is designed to increase the value you can obtain from your SAP BI platform. It engages users to enter their knowledge and expertise via the BI mini apps. The BI mini apps are comprised of specialized user knowledge packaged in the form of an analytical BI mini app. However, how can the need for a BI mini app be captured? How can it be determined that there is a gap between the expertise that users have and the way the system functionality is leveraged? A significant part of this process is analyzing the existing SAP ECC system.

The utilization analysis is based on common system audit procedures. This portion of the analysis can drive more productivity in the system.

What is utilization analysis?

 Utilization analysis uses audit features that are built into the functions and tables used with a given instance of SAP. Within constraints given by the SAP system size and deployment, this approach can assist with the definition of an adequate reporting layer.

The SAP audit features track the use of the system. The technique allows you to reference the tables used by the transactions and then appropriate this information to determine how the system is used versus its intended use. In addition, the information collected forms one of the building blocks to dynamically generate a reporting system.

Let's briefly review the different ways to audit SAP system usage. I will cover the different system usage types via transaction code, function module, table access, and BAPIs. This way, you as the reader will understand the options you have available to interact with SAP. It will clarify the scope and limitations in later chapters where I will utilize direct table access for reporting. How does it clarify and limit the scope? Based on the system utilization audit, it can be determined what transaction codes the users are employing. This determines and limits the data model that is relevant for the reporting strategy.

3.2   Different ways to conduct system audits

System audit concepts are used to prove compliance based on industry requirements. However, in this scenario, I am using it to document how the system is used and to drive relevant improvements. The key factors to analyze are:

► What transaction codes are employed by users during their work days?

► What transaction codes are available to users based on the roles assigned to them?

Based on this information, conclusions can be drawn that are relevant for BI reporting, user training, and system customization.

3.2.1 SAP BI reporting conclusions

Once the transaction codes and reports employed by a user are determined, it is possible to evaluate if the way the system is used adequately supports the business processes that are handled by the user. If, for example, the user group does not utilize implemented reports and instead continues to employ custom reports in Excel, then there is a high likelihood that additional system training is required alongside the need for translating the custom report into a BI mini app with the relevant reporting information included.

Furthermore, the transaction code utilization also determines the relevant data model for the particular SAP ECC system.

3.2.2 User training conclusions

In addition, the transaction code and report usage can provide insights into discrepancies between the system features and how the system is used. Relevant user groups may require re-training in cases where features are available but remain unused.

3.2.3 System customization conclusions

Often, powerful features in SAP ECC remain unused because, during the initial implementation phase, a go-live date had to be achieved, and the infamous Phase 2 tasks were never implemented. For example, Material Requirements Planning (MRP) is a candidate for this. MRP functionality is included with SAP ECC, but remains unused in many systems. These types of areas can be identified with the transaction code analysis. Therefore, the transaction code analysis can also lead to new blueprint definition requirements. With regards to MRP, this may consequently lead to a corporate MRP Production Planning blueprint.

3.3 Transaction code analysis concept

The transaction code utilization audit can be done using various approaches in SAP ECC. This is not uncommon with SAP ECC, as there are various angles you can approach the system from. For example, while in some instances you may want to use a transaction code to get the relevant information, you may find that you want to collect data over time to drive detailed analytics against the data, which is sometimes not initially possible using a transaction code. In this instance, you may opt for a BAPI interface that uses a set of BAPIs from within the SAP system against selected instances. In addition, the available tools in SAP are constantly changing and being improved, and there is a good chance that you may find a different tool in SAP Solution Manager that may promise to resolve the task. However, keep in mind that the true value from the SAP ECC system comes from the very core of it. Consequently, you can always count on the ability to get the job done using transaction codes and BAPIs, which is exactly what those other tools available in Solution Manager are doing. In addition, the more you learn about the SAP ECC system, the more you will find out that many features that are available via new SAP products were already built into the core SAP ECC system. For example, BI, MRP, and forecasting and web services to connect with external systems are part of SAP ECC.

3.4 How to use ST03n, SM19, and SM20

There are various methods available for auditing the system. However, the best option to identify what transaction codes a user has employed is to run the SAP transaction ST03n. This will open the Workload Monitor. You will have to activate EXPERT MODE.

As shown in Figure 3.1, once you have ST03n open, select TOTAL and then USER AND SETTLEMENT STATISTICS. In the submenu, select USER PROFILES. Within this transaction, there is also an alternate method you can reach via choosing TOTAL and then selecting BUSINESS TRANSACTION ANALYSIS. This will then show the same result that you would get via the STAD transaction code.

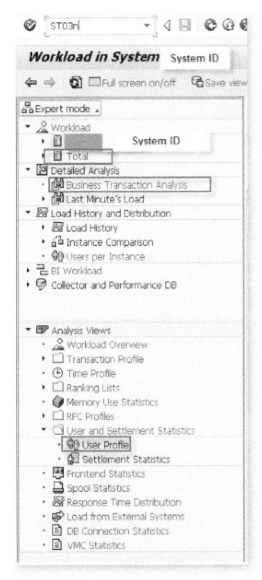

Figure 3.1: Transaction code ST03n

Figure 3.2 shows the transaction codes used in this system in the TRANS-ACTION column. In order to activate the system log file to continuously capture required log information, I will utilize transaction SM19 (see Figure 3.3), which allows me to configure the type of data that will be collected.

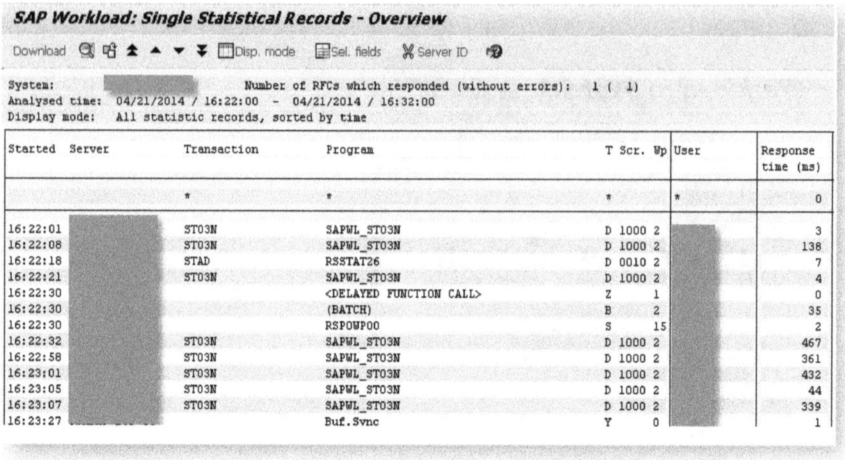

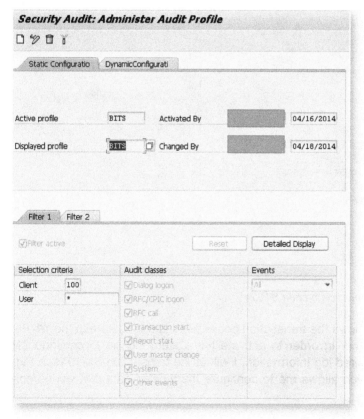

Figure 3.2: STAD or ST03N via business transaction analysis

Figure 3.3: Transaction code SM19—create audit profile

The audit profile has options for filtering out only those events that you want to track in the auditing process.

In this example, I have activated all of the criteria. In Figure 3.4, you see the area REREAD AUDIT LOG. This allows you to read the current audit log and view the results. This is identical to the area described in ST03n, which shows the same result as STAD.

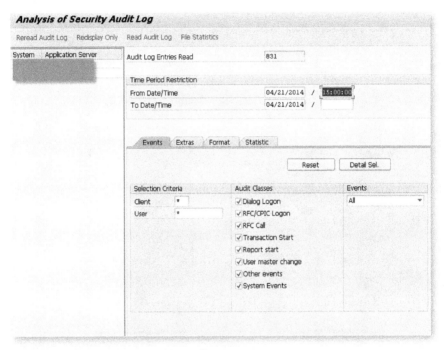

Figure 3.4: Configure audit profile options

If you want to identify the location of the audit files, use the top menu path GOTO • FILE LIST as shown in Figure 3.5.

Figure 3.5: Find file location of audit log files

Once you click on RE-READ AUDIT LOG or call the STAD transaction, then you will see a result similar to the one shown in Figure 3.6. The TRANSACTION column shows the transaction codes used by users. Note that this analysis also shows the PROGRAM, which is an essential part of our later effort to develop the custom data model for this particular SAP ECC implementation.

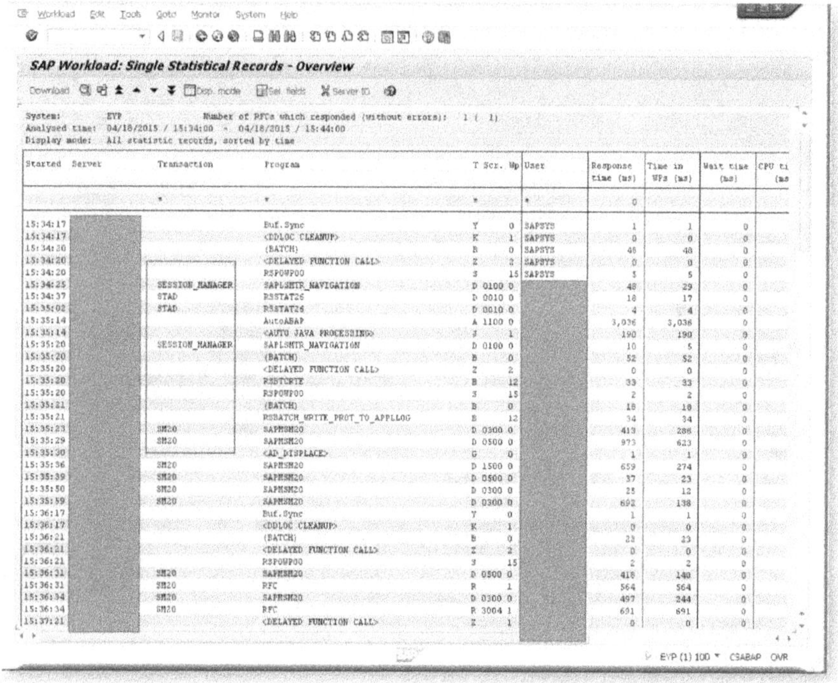

Figure 3.6: SM20 shows the transaction code when you read the log files

Transaction code SM20 reads the log file content and allows you to view the content. Now that the relevant information is available, the process needs to be automated.

There is a program in SAP that can be executed and return the results seen when running the transaction code STAD. It is called RSAU SELECT EVENTS and is a report built into SAP ECC. It allows you to obtain the information I discussed above via a report. For these purposes, the report needs to be automated so that it runs every day and exports the data to a database automatically. It is possible to do this, but it is not a very straightforward process.

You can run reports and programs manually using transaction code SE38. Once you run the report, you can schedule it via SM36.

Figure 3.7: Transaction code SE38—Run ABAP report

In order to automate this process using the ABAP report RSAU_SELECT_EVENTS, the report can be scheduled via transaction code SM36.The process involves writing the file to a spooler and then grabbing the spooler file via BAPI RSPO_DOWNLOAD_SPOOLJOB. In addition, I have to add a variant input variable when I schedule the report because I need to run the report with dynamic data ranges.

To summarize the method outlined above, the following steps need to be completed to get the SAP utilization information:

SM19 • SM20 • SM36 • VARIANT • SPOOLER • BAPI "RSPO _DOWNLOAD_SPOOLJOB

This process seems rather convoluted and is not efficient. In addition, data obtained this way must also be collected in a database. This is required to analyze trends, etc. Let's take a look at two alternate methods. While I was able to produce the required results with the previous method, it is very complex to automate the process and utilize the information in an external database for reporting. Therefore, I suggest alternate approaches to better run and automate the process.

3.5   Using BAPIs to extract utilization data

It is one thing to run a transaction code with a transaction. It is another story to automate the process to retrieve data that is ready for analysis.

As shown in Section 3.4, a series of transaction codes can only be used for ad hoc analysis. In order to automate the process, there is a simpler, more straightforward approach.

What is a BAPI?

 The SAP ECC system offers BAPIS. BAPIS are Business APIs (BAPI). The acronym BAPI stands for Business Application Programming Interface.

In fact, it is notable that a large part of the functionality in SAP can be utilized without the SAP GUI, but rather using BAPIs. I will utilize a BAPI to extract the required utilization data and write it into an external database where the data can be used to analyze trends.

There is a transaction code in SAP that allows you to test and run a BAPI. This way, you can identify what input data is required, and you can determine if the result meets your goal. In this case, we will utilize transaction code SE37 (see Figure 3.8). This allows you to run BAPIs and provide the same input that you would later provide in your own application. SAP provides various BAPIs focused on system utilization and statistical data analysis. Once you have SE37 open, you can enter the name of the BAPI SWNC_COLLECTOR_GET_AGGREGATES.

When you run this BAPI with the correct parameters, you will see the result tables. In Figure 3.9, see the highlighted area USERTCODE. It shows 36 records. If you click on the icon next to 36 ENTRIES, you can see the details for each entry.

Figure 3.8: BAPI runner SE37

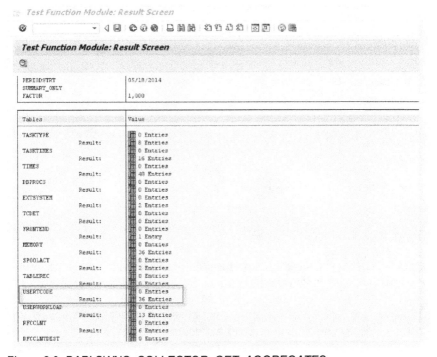

Figure 3.9: BAPI SWNC_COLLECTOR_GET_AGGREGATES

The BAPI SWNC_COLLECTOR_GET_AGGREGATES uses the table MONI on the database table level. You may think that you can just query this table directly. However, in SAP, there are various types of tables that cannot be used the same way as regular SQL database tables. The MONI table is a table with cluster columns. This means that metadata is stored here, which is used by the application server to get the actual data dynamically.

Therefore, you cannot get data via direct table access. You have to use the BAPI to extract the data.

You can evaluate the structure of the MONI table using transaction code SE11 (see Figure 3.10).

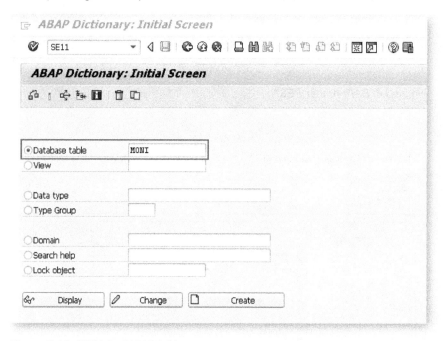

Figure 3.10: SE11 for MONI table

Click on DISPLAY to view the structure of the MONI table, which will reveal that it is a cluster table (actually cluster column) as shown in Figure 3.11.

Tables in the SAP database may have cluster columns. In this case, you cannot directly use SQL queries to extract the information.

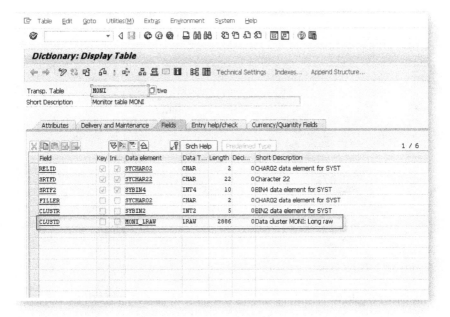

Figure 3.11: MONI table structure

In the meantime, I have gathered the required information to run and test BAPIs. With this information, you can now use SAP GUI to test the parameters needed to produce the required output for your application. In this case, I used the SWNC_COLLECTOR_GET_AGGREGATES function module to get the required statistical information based on transaction code use.

3.6   Automating BAPIs without programming

In order to run BAPIs, you need to define the interface and programmatically provide the data via C++ or ABAP programs. However, I am using a solution that enables the user to first find a BAPI, then identify the interface elements and finally, provide the required input data via a graphical user interface. The solution is called BITS and leverages BAPIs.

The BITS interface shows a graphical interface where you can organize your tasks and design the workflow. The green boxes represent direct table access. The yellow boxes are BAPIs that take input and produce output (see Figure 3.12).

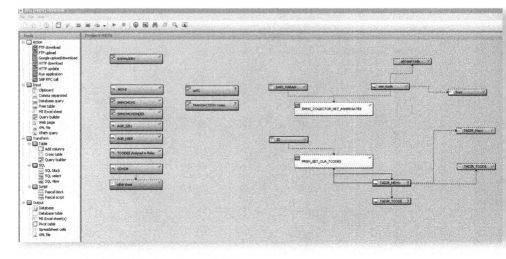

Figure 3.12: BITS interface to run BAPIs

The BAPI explorer interface allows the user to search a BAPI by keyword and then view the interface elements. This essentially provides the functionality available via SE37. You can search, find, and test BAPIs using this interface. In Figure 3.13, you can see the BAPI I searched for and the required input fields, just like you see in SAP SE37. However, now you can work without the SAP GUI to automate the task.

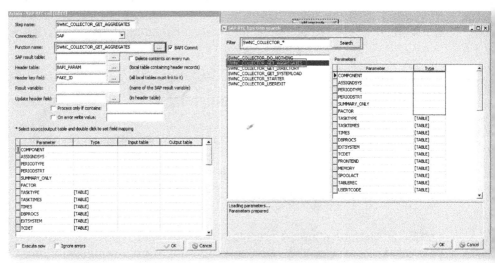

Figure 3.13: BITS BAPI explorer

Using this concept in BITS, you can easily automate data extraction from SAP ECC using BAPIs and function modules. Later in this book, I will further expand on this approach and will use BITS to drive the SAP data model to build the platform for SAP BI Edge.

3.7   The most important SAP transaction codes revealed

Using system utilization analysis has provided us with information about the relevant transaction codes, BAPIs, and tables such as MONI. However, how can you connect all of this information without prior knowledge of the inner workings of your SAP system?

With the following concept, you can understand the SAP system and structure the relations of tables, procedures, etc. In the SAP GUI, enter SE93. This transaction code allows you to maintain transactions. For example, you can enter the transaction VA02 and click on DISPLAY (see Figure 3.14). The result will show the transaction name CHANGE SALES ORDER. You can also just enter a * in the transaction code form field. Then you can press F4 to see the full list of transaction codes by description and transaction code. Note that because there are a lot of transaction codes, this list will only show a filtered preview. However, for now, you may understand the key value of SE93. The subsequent screen also shows the PROGRAM NAME that is used internally by SAP to run VA02.

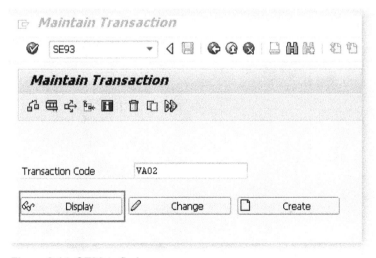

Figure 3.14: SE93 to find program name

The program name is displayed in the DISPLAY DIALOG TRANSACTION screen. We can use this program name to find the relevant dictionary objects and tables using SE80, which is the ABAP Workbench.

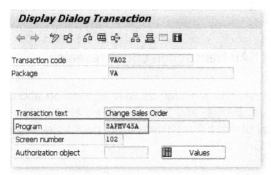

Figure 3.15: SE93 showing the program name

In essence, this is a way to identify all of the tables involved in certain SAP transactions (see Figure 3.16).

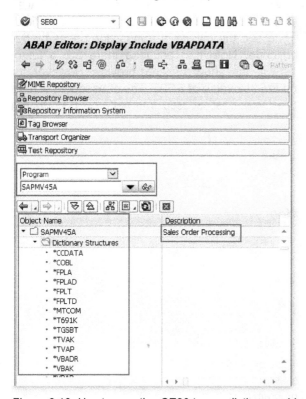

Figure 3.16: Use transaction SE80 to see dictionary object and tables

3.7.1   System Audit Concept Overview

▶ Use the SAP BAPI that collects auditing information to automatically obtain transaction codes used by users.

▶ When reviewing the transaction codes, also make note of the program names associated with the transactions.

▶ Use SE80 to list the data dictionary tables used by program names.

▶ Use this information to define the data model that is relevant for your ECC system. You can do this by tracking the transaction code and the related program names, which you then can review in the data dictionary.

▶ Use BITS to generate the data model and automate the process. This way, you do not have to go through the process noted above manually.

▶ Use BITS to write data back using BAPIs. This allows you to interact with SAP and write data back instead of just reading it for reporting. This can be important if you interface with an e-commerce platform, for example. You would read the relevant product information and use it to update your ecommerce. Then you would return and write the sales orders back into SAP.

In order to better utilize this concept, keep in mind that SAP transaction codes have a common structure. The suffix "1" usually indicates that this transaction code is used to create transaction data. The suffix "2" is used to indicate that the relevant transaction code is used to change already existing transactional data. I have noted a rough categorization of this concept below. You can use this information to better identify the relevant tables. You can also group the tables involved using this filter.

SAP transaction code structure:

▶ XX01 ⇨ Create
▶ XX02 ⇨ Change
▶ XX03 ⇨ Display

3.8   From SAP data to report

In order to efficiently create reports using BI Edge tools, it is important to understand the inner structure of your SAP ECC system. Due to the complexity of the SAP ERP system, there can be very different structures in place with regard to tables and data, depending on your SAP configuration. Therefore, the SAP system audit method has been established to analyze the system and determine how it is used by users.

Furthermore, users can uncover untapped potential by identifying SAP functionalities that are available but remain unused. With this concept, reports can now be created against SAP ECC.

To summarize these efforts, see Figure 3.17 for an overview chart of the tools I used in this chapter. You can use it as a guide for your own project.

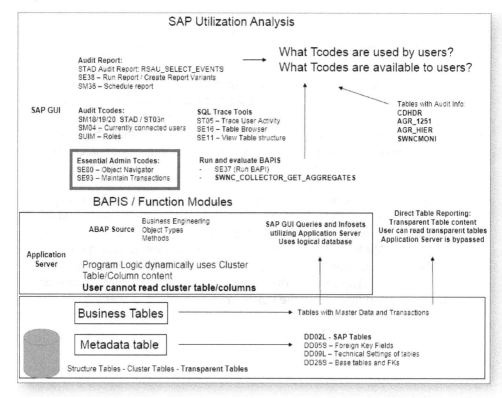

Figure 3.17: SAP audit overview

Figure 3.17 shows the path your data takes from the lower database level where data is stored in tables. The tables can be used in direct queries, and in that case, are called transparent tables. Cluster tables have content that will be prepared by the application server once read. Therefore, the user cannot query this data directly. In order to find tables with information, you can use transaction code analysis and auditing. Using transaction codes will allow you to determine the tables used in SAP. You will use SE93 and SE80 to do this. The relevant dictionary information is the basis for your custom SAP data model, which we will further explore in the Chapter 4.

4 Connecting to SAP ECC 6.0

When writing reports against SAP ECC, it is critical to identify the relevant information objects. In order to accomplish this task, a data model is most commonly used. However, with SAP ECC, the underlying data model is so complex that it is not available in a simple format. The data models you can obtain are usually oversimplified, too complex, or not accurate. The reason for this is that SAP ECC has thousands of tables, and based on the configuration, there may be different table structures.

In addition, not all tables are meant to be read by the user directly. To recap, SAP uses different table types to store data. The different table types are:

- ▶ Structure tables.
- ▶ Cluster tables.
- ▶ Transparent tables.

When I say that SAP has a lot of tables, it is really true. There are more than 50,000 tables in a standard SAP ECC system. However, users can only employ the transparent tables for queries. The structure and cluster tables are used by the SAP application server to assemble data dynamically as the user works with SAP via the GUI or another interface.

Keep in mind, though, that all the tables are rarely needed to obtain meaningful transaction data. Most SAP systems use a common set of functionalities. The common areas are grouped by the modules that are configured for that particular SAP system. The subtle variances in configuration make all the difference when trying to get your queries to run with SAP ECC. Those will be captured with transaction code utilization.

These subtle differences can have a significant impact. Some examples of configuration-specific settings that vary from system to system are:

- ▶ Specific pricing conditions to configure how pricing is applied in sales orders.

▶ Localized tax settings can have a big impact on how tax calculations are done. They may be different from country to country and can sometimes also be undocumented. I mention this because, in some smaller countries in Eastern Europe, the tax requirements are unique and are often adapted by local experts. Depending on how fast the relevant laws and regulations change, the relevant tables, programs, etc. may be undocumented.

Therefore, I dynamically develop the data model on a per-system basis. The steps taken to develop the data model are the following:

▶ Determine transaction codes used in SAP system based on SAP utilization analysis.

▶ Determine the programs associated with transaction codes.

▶ Determine the tables used by these programs using the ABAP Workbench.

▶ Use this information to create a dynamic repository.

▶ Develop data models based on the repository.

Please note that this concept can be entirely automated up to the point that you generate the repository. In this book, I am using N2ONE Bits to accomplish these tasks. But, what if this approach does not get you to the information you need? In this case, you can use the concept of SQL tracing.

4.1   The repository concept and KPIs

As part of BI Edge, you get the tools to connect with SAP ECC. Whatever tools you use to collect the data, it is important to keep in mind the destination and the potential user group. Hence, the data sources you create have multiple layers. In SAP BI Edge, these layers are represented in the universe concept via the data layer, the semantic layer, and the business layer.

However, the BI Edge tools provide no direct support to simplify query generation with direct table access. In addition, we cannot write data back to SAP ECC, which could be required in some instances. In order to achieve this task, you need additional SAP products. An alternative solution for this is, once again, N2ONE Bits, which I will continue to use to generate the external data model.

In the meantime, I will further focus on the tools provided by SAP in SAP ECC. As I mentioned before, the SAP ECC system already includes many tools. In fact, the more you learn about SAP, the more you will realize that many products that evolved from SAP to address certain market needs already existed in SAP R/3 and SAP ECC. This fact also leads to the conclusion that a bare bones SAP ECC system is often a better choice than having additional products in the solution architecture.

Therefore, I will focus on the query tools that are built in with SAP ECC. You can use these query tools to create direct table queries, create queries against the logical database, etc. These tools are important because you can use them as a data source in SAP BI Edge.

The concepts explained in this chapter are essential when it comes to designing the BI Edge universes. The BI Edge universes hold the information architecture from the data source to report in a file. With this in mind, you can better understand why InfoSets in SAP can be used as a data source in SAP BI Edge in the universe concept.

I will discuss the benefits and limitations of these tools in this chapter. In addition, I will add more information to the case study, which will continue to describe the steps required to develop and fine-tune your own database model with SAP ECC access.

4.2   The SAP InfoSet concept

To get started with SAP queries in SAP ECC, use the transaction code SQVI to open the QuickViewer. It is, in essence, it is a landing page for all of your SAP queries.

Figure 4.1: SQVI QuickViewer initial screen

In Figure 4.1, you can see that there are two main sections of the screen. On the left side, there is a brief explanation of the features available in this section. As discussed previously, most SAP transaction codes are categorized by a suffix, which identifies the purpose of the transaction code with regards to create, change, and view functionality. In this case, the relevant transaction codes are available via the links on the main SQVI page. For example, if you click on SAP QUERY, you will go to a new screen, which you can also reach directly using transaction code SQ01 (create). The other relevant transaction codes are SQ02 and SQ03.

The suffixes 01- 03 in the context of queries mean:

- ▶ SQ01: Create SAP Query.
- ▶ SQ02: InfoSet based on SAP Query.
- ▶ SQ03: Assign user groups who can use an InfoSet.

You can see that the increasing suffix identifier structures the expected workflow. I designed the query, then I assigned a query to an InfoSet. Finally, I assigned a security context for the InfoSet.

4.3   SAP InfoSets explained

Based on the description above, you can see that an InfoSet uses a query, which then can be employed by users who have access to the security context assigned to the InfoSet. In other words, you can only run an InfoSet if you have the proper privileges. This is a crucial detail because I will utilize InfoSets as data sources for BI Edge later in this book. Therefore, you can see that the data we use in BI Edge can be defined in SAP ECC using query tools that are already built in to your core SAP ECC system. The execution of InfoSets outside of SAP require that the user executing them have the relevant privileges assigned. The new BI Edge version includes a new option that allows the user to connect with SAP ECC using InfoSets. For this reason, you can utilize this concept to create Crystal Reports in BI Edge. If you already have preexisting queries and InfoSets, you can also leverage this fact and use them in Crystal Reports as a data source. However, as mentioned previously, you need to make sure that the relevant user has the required privileges.

4.4   SQ01/SQ02/SQ03

To design a basic query in SAP ECC, start by using transaction code SQ01. In the example in Figure 4.2, you can see that I will be creating a query called N2ONE_SOs. In essence, I will be creating a query that shows all the sales orders and delivery information.

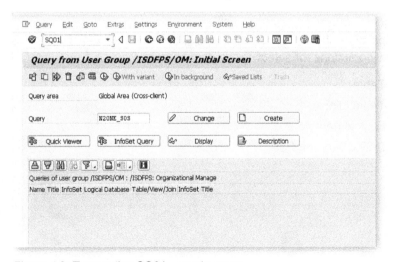

Figure 4.2: Transaction SQ01—create query

Before I continue to create a query, I will briefly review the other transaction codes involved in this process. Transaction SQ02 transaction allows you to create an InfoSet, which you can do by assigning a query and the security context (see Figure 4.3).

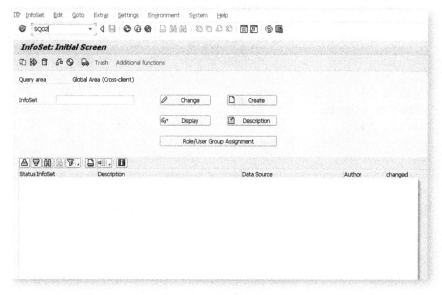

Figure 4.3: Transaction SQ02—InfoSet initial screen

Transaction code SQ03 is the interface for the user to create and assign security limitations and groups for the InfoSet (see Figure 4.4).

With this in mind, I can continue with the query creation process by selecting the type of data source that I will utilize. In SAP ECC, you have the following options for selecting the data source:

▶ Table.

▶ Table join.

▶ Logical database.

▶ SAP Query InfoSet.

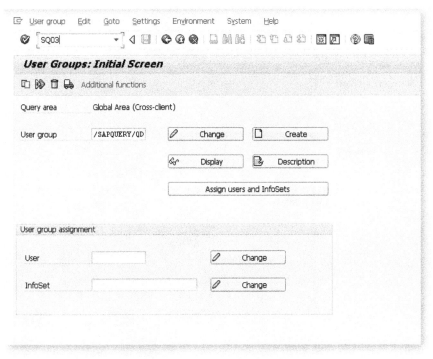

Figure 4.4: Transaction SQ03—query security context

4.4.1 Table data source

The table data source allows you to specify a single table, which can then be used in the query. Naturally, this does not allow for a lot of flexibility because you are limited to a single table. This data source is geared toward situations where users may have used transaction code SE16, which allows you to view the content of a specified table. Use the transaction code SQVI to create queries, create an InfoSet based on the query, and then make the same information that was available via SE16 available in Crystal Reports. In this scenario, the user would have to use the InfoSet as a data source in Crystal Reports (see Figure 4.5).

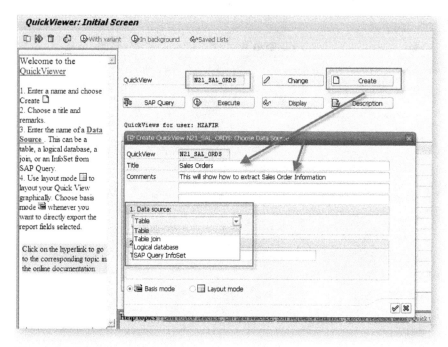

Figure 4.5: SQVI data sources

4.4.2 Table join

The *table join data source* is where the real fun starts when it comes to creating your own queries. Use this data source to add related tables and connect their columns based on primary and foreign keys. In the following sections, I will briefly walk through this option. You will learn how to add related tables, understand how they connect, and verify the connections.

4.4.3 Logical database

The *logical database data source* hides the complexity of the underlying table connections with primary keys and foreign keys from the user. Instead, you can choose the type of information you want to retrieve from a functional point of view. For example, you can choose a logical database that holds sales order information. You then do not have to worry about the details. You can assume that you will find sales order information in the logical database.

4.4.4 SAP Query InfoSet

The *InfoSet data source* can be viewed as a type of logical database data source because it may incorporate the logic to obtain sales order information or other information that is organized based on the type of transactions. However, the InfoSet also includes the authorization limits that come with the InfoSet privileges.

4.4.5 How to use a table join

If you looked closely at the data source options, you may have noticed that the table join option is the most powerful option, but also the most challenging one. It gives you the most control and therefore requires that you also know what you are doing. I will take you through a closer look at this option and go through an actual example.

Once you have selected the data source TABLE JOIN, you will see an empty area with an icon-based menu system (see Figure 4.6). Select INSERT TABLE. Select carefully because it is advisable to connect tables from left to right. In fact, if you do not follow this paradigm, the system may give you an error when you check the validity of the connections.

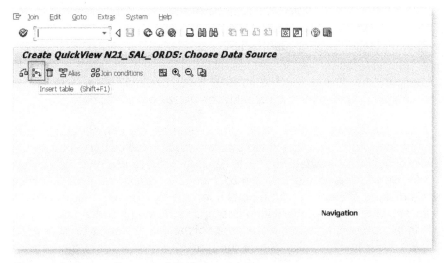

Figure 4.6: Transaction code SQVI—insert tables

In this example, I have selected the tables in the following sequence:

- ▶ VBAK "Sales Document Header Data"
- ▶ VBAP "Sales Document Item Data"
- ▶ KNA1 "General Data Customer Master"
- ▶ LIPS "SO Documents: Delivery: Item Data"
- ▶ LIKP "SO Documents: Delivery: Header"
- ▶ VBRP "Billing Document: Item Data"
- ▶ VBRK "Billing Document: Header Data"

These are transparent tables that hold business data. The tables are connected with key fields called *primary keys* and *foreign keys*. For example, the VBAK table holds sales document header information. The primary key in this table is the VBELN (evolved from the German word Beleg Nummer) column. This table connects with the VBELN column in the VBAP table, which holds the item data of the sales orders. Subsequently, all the tables are connected by single key columns or a combination of key columns. The relevant logic must be developed based on business logic and required target result.

Please note that the core transaction tables are the same for all SAP ECC systems. However, there may be subtle differences based on how the system is configured. For example, when you create a query to get sales orders and pricing for items, then you will have to consider that different tables may contain the relevant data based on how the particular pricing system was implemented. VK13 is the transaction code to configure the pricing structure in SAP ECC. Depending how this pricing structure is implemented, different types of tables hold the data.

When you add the tables in the right sequence, the primary and foreign key connections are made for you automatically. You can also update the join conditions by selecting the tables you want to join and then select JOIN CONDITIONS in the icon based menu. An additional aspect makes this method of creating your reports user friendly is that the table name is accompanied by the table's long description. When I mention user friendly in this context, I mean that the intent of the design seems to have been to be "user friendly." You decide for yourself if that is really the case or not.

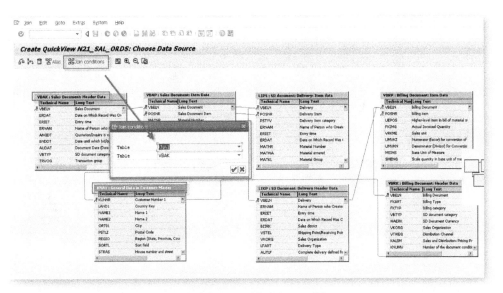

Figure 4.7: Transaction code SQVI —table join conditions

As you add more tables and connect them, you may come across a situation where there are multiple columns that have to combine to achieve a proper link. In this scenario, it can get complex quickly, and you may have trouble managing the complexity. I recommend that you create a group of manageable queries and table links and then combine those to create a query hierarchy.

The SAP ECC table join manager also assists with this issue with the CHECK TABLE JOIN CONDITIONS feature. Interestingly, this feature checks the join conditions from left to right. Therefore, the way the tables are organized on the screen has an impact on how the logic is tested. For example, in this scenario, there is a message that indicates TABLE LIKP MUST BE THE RIGHT HAND TABLE IN A JOIN (see Figure 4.8). While this is rather counterintuitive, it can actually be helpful at times.

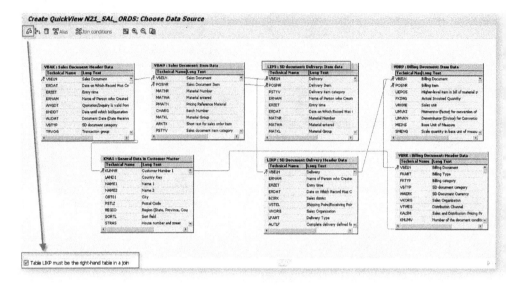

Figure 4.8: Transaction code SQVI—check table join conditions

Once the table is moved a bit to the right, the TABLE JOIN checking feature approves (see Figure 4.9).

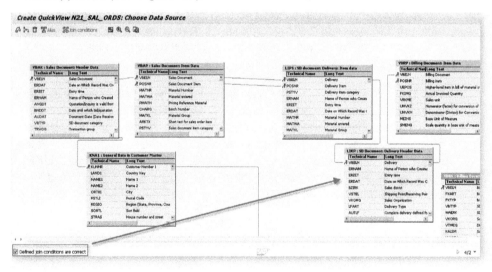

Figure 4.9: Transaction code SQVI —table joins positioning

Without consideration of the positional impact of a table, I have grouped the tables in this example query by function. You can use this as a starting point for your own sales order queries. The functional groups of tables are the essential order-to-cash (OTC) tables and are surrounded by red boxes (see Figure 4.10).

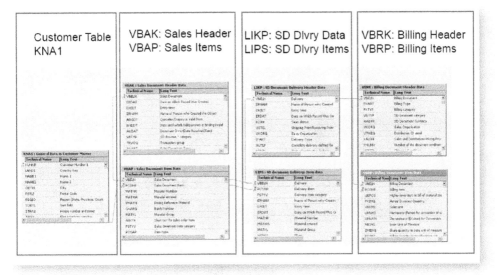

Figure 4.10: Direct table example logic

Once all the tables you require for your query are selected and connected properly, you can proceed with the next step. Select the columns from the selected tables that you want to display in the query result. Keep in mind that, up until now, you only selected the tables, and the logical way they are connected is by Primary Keys (PKs) and Foreign Keys (FKs). Now you can select the relevant columns. This is achieved by reviewing the DATA FIELDS section in the top left corner. Once you click on the arrow next to the table name, all of the columns for this table will be displayed, and you can select them. The selected columns will be displayed in the right hand section FIELDS IN LIST (see Figure 4.11).

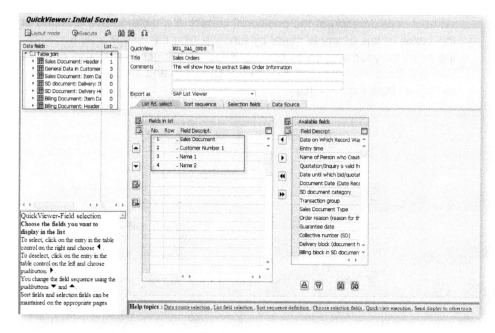

Figure 4.11: Transaction code SQVI—manage columns for report

In this example in Figure 4.11, I have CUSTOMER NUMBER 1, NAME 1, and NAME 2 selected. If you carefully review the other tab pages on the right, you can conclude that the subsequent steps would involve sorting, etc. Therefore, you can essentially create a customized query using the table-based tools available in SAP ECC.

In other words, this is a visual query designer where the forms and fields completed will determine the resulting query logic (see Figure 4.12).

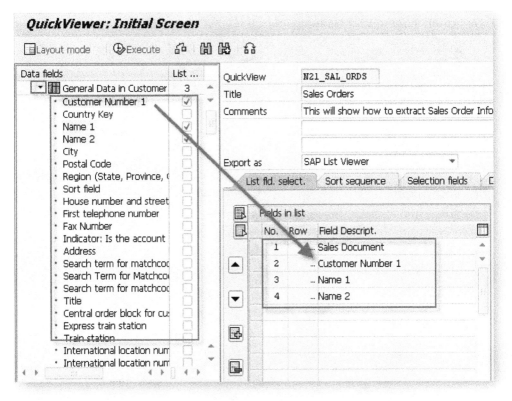

Figure 4.12: Transaction code SQVI—selected columns

You can also test the query as you progress through the process. Once you test it, you can save the query. To initiate the test, click on the EXE-CUTE button as shown in Figure 4.13.

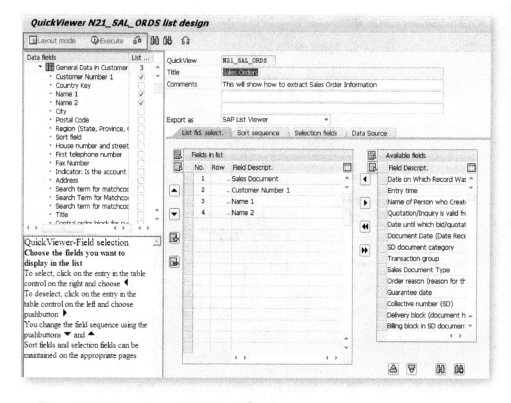

Figure 4.13: Transaction code SQVI – test run

Figure 4.14 shows the additional options available to design the query using table-based forms in SAP ECC.

The last step in the process will save the query with the name you assign. By doing so, you can call this query again later using the parameters you defined. With reference to SAP BI Edge, this means that the query will be available in Crystal Reports only if you create an InfoSet based on the query (see Figure 4.15).

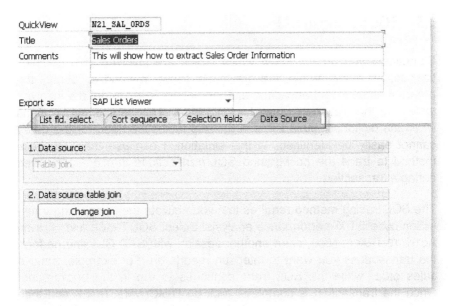

Figure 4.14: Transaction code SQVI—additional options

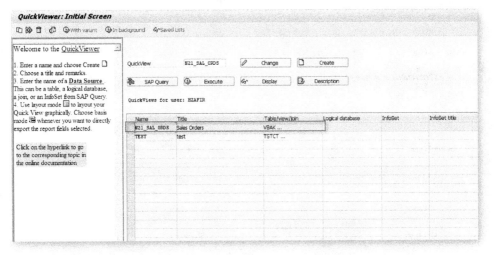

Figure 4.15: Save the query so that it appears in the query list

4.5 SQL tracing in SAP

Sometimes you do not know which tables are involved in a complex transaction. For example, the previously shown method to identify the program name for a transaction and then using SE80 to get the involved tables via the dictionary view does not work. This sometimes happens when the dictionary table list is large, and tables we need for the query cannot easily be identified. In this situation, I can use the *SQL trace* method to trace the background SQL transactions that are performed during a transaction.

The SQL tracing method requires that you activate the trace using transaction code ST05 performance analysis. Select SQL TRACE and click on ACTIVATE TRACE. Next, open another session with SAP GUI and perform the transactions you want to later run reports on. For example, enter a sales order while the SQL trace continues to run in the background. Once the transaction is complete, click on DEACTIVATE TRACE and then run DISPLAY TRACE. The trace collected contains all of the SQL transactions performed by the transaction (see Figure 4.16).

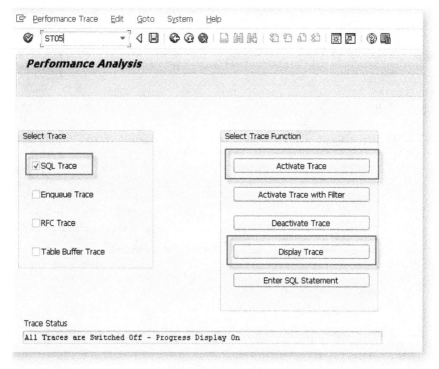

Figure 4.16: Transaction code ST05 – tracing SQL

In the trace window, click on the line that relates to the transaction you want to analyze. Then, in the top section, select EXPLAIN. In SQL terms, this means that the SQL transactions are explained in detailed SQL notation. Essentially, you get all of the SQL commands that were performed during the SAP transactions while the SQL trace was active. In other words, by analyzing the SQL commands, you can reverse-engineer the SAP transactions and identify the tables that were used to write the data during the transaction. Hence, you get the relevant tables and the primary key and foreign key relationships most of the time. If you utilize this method, you will also understand that there are often many transactions in SAP ECC that are not relevant for a specific SQL trace. Therefore, you need to develop a good understanding of which record to select in the trace window. In addition, you have to adequately set the proper filters when you start the trace (see Figure 4.17).

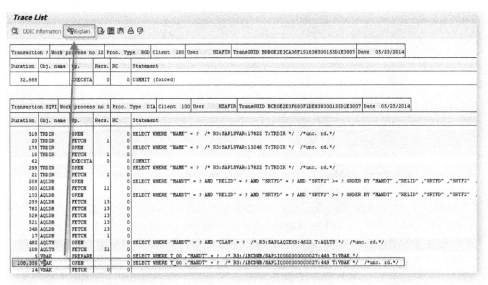

Figure 4.17: Trace list explain SQL details

When you identify the correct record and click EXPLAIN, then you will get a full SQL statement (see Figure 4.18). In summary, you can use the information to:

▶ Identify tables used during SAP transactions.

▶ Identify the relationship between the tables.

▶ Review columns used by the tables.

▶ Identify the possible use of non-transparent tables.

▶ Review the parameters used to filter the result set.

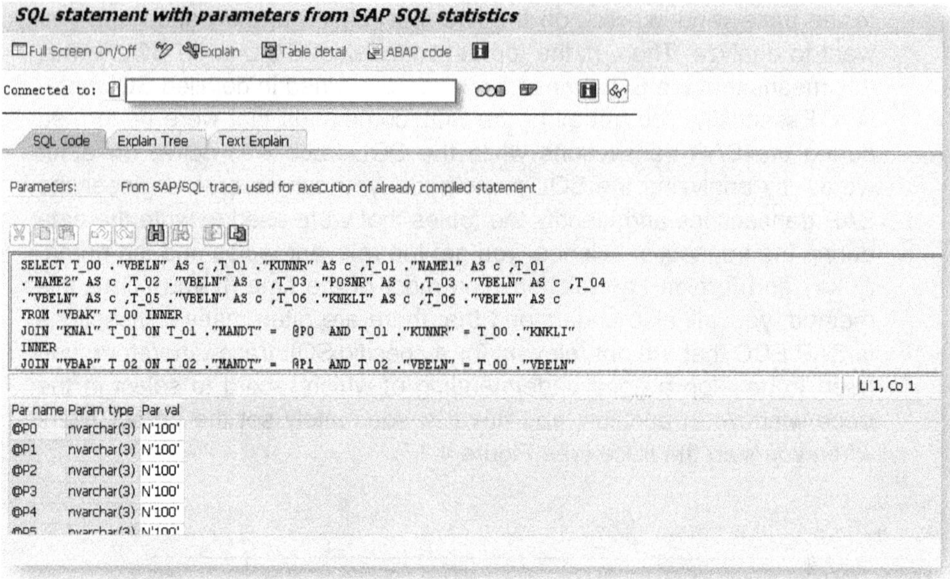

SQL statement with parameters from SAP SQL statistics

☐ Full Screen On/Off ✏️ 🔍Explain 📋 Table detail 📄 ABAP code ℹ️

Connected to: ☐ [   ] CO0 🖥️   ℹ️ 🔧

| SQL Code | Explain Tree | Text Explain |

Parameters: From SAP/SQL trace, used for execution of already compiled statement

✂️🗐🖫 🔁🔂 🔖🔗 🗎🗐

```
SELECT T_00 ."VBELN" AS c ,T_01 ."KUNNR" AS c ,T_01 ."NAME1" AS c ,T_01
."NAME2" AS c ,T_02 ."VBELN" AS c ,T_03 ."POSNR" AS c ,T_03 ."VBELN" AS c ,T_04
."VBELN" AS c ,T_05 ."VBELN" AS c ,T_06 ."KNKLI" AS c ,T_06 ."VBELN" AS c
FROM "VBAK" T_00 INNER
JOIN "KNA1" T_01 ON T_01 ."MANDT" = @P0 AND T_01 ."KUNNR" = T_00 ."KNKLI"
INNER
JOIN "VBAP" T_02 ON T_02 ."MANDT" = @P1 AND T_02 ."VBELN" = T_00 ."VBELN"
```
                                                                    Li 1, Co 1

Par name	Param type	Par val
@P0	nvarchar(3)	N'100'
@P1	nvarchar(3)	N'100'
@P2	nvarchar(3)	N'100'
@P3	nvarchar(3)	N'100'
@P4	nvarchar(3)	N'100'
@P5	nvarchar(3)	N'100'

Figure 4.18: SQL explain details

Therefore, you can use the SAP GUI to run the transactions you want to report on. Enable the trace and then analyze the trace result using the method described above.

As this task may evolve into a tedious process to go through all of the tables and identify their name, columns, and links to other tables, I recommend an organized approach. For example, if you want to trace a single transaction, you can easily use the method suggested here. However, if you have a large set of transactions, it requires that you organize and structure the project.

An example tool you can use to organize the queries and data in a way so that you can easily maintain it and use it in BI Edge is the N2ONE Bits SQL Designer for SAP ECC. This tool is built in with the core N2ONE Bits interface. You can easily find a table by its table name and then see the table description and the links to other tables. It makes the task of going through many SAP transaction codes with multiple sessions much easier and reduces it to a single interface where you can immediately test and adjust your queries even without a SAP connection (see Figure 4.19).

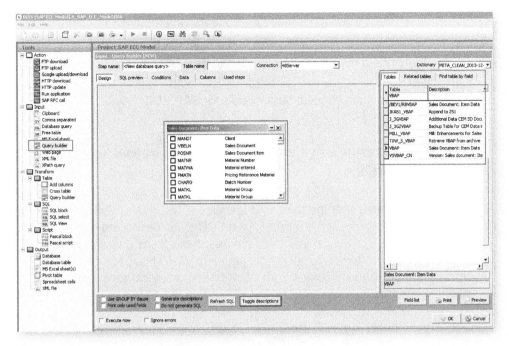

Figure 4.19: BITS SAP ECC Query Designer

In Figure 4.19, you can see the table VBAP selected on the right side. I can easily identify the table using a direct table search or by entering a search key for the table description. This searches the SAP table repository and returns a list of matching candidates. You can drag the desired table to the center and then continue with related tables. You can also generate descriptive documentation that makes the resulting code easy to read. This is especially important when you design complex queries and need to update them or have third party team members who need to make updates to existing queries. Please also note that you can further add BAPI integrations to obtain data from SAP ECC based on transactions.

With this method, I can:

▶ Easily create SAP ECC queries.

▶ Document the results in the Query Tool.

▶ Structure queries hierarchically to keep them simple.

▶ Enable team members to modify queries.

77

▶ Use BAPIs to obtain transaction code use information.

▶ Generate a transaction code cloud and landscape automatically.

▶ Identify the tables used in the department or company automatically.

▶ Implement customized data models for SAP ECC.

4.6 Your company's dynamic data model and transaction code portfolio

You are now armed with the tools and techniques to conquer every SAP reporting challenge using the existing SAP ECC tools. Combined with the additional tool N2ONE Bits, you can leverage these steps and automate transaction code utilization. With the standard SAP business models, which are organized by business function based on modules, you have all of the required information needed for your specific project.

SAP has standard transaction tables that are used to collect business transactions. Based on your specific configuration, collect the transaction codes used by department. Using the concepts presented in this book, you can identify the tables used for the transactions. Given the nature of the tables involved, you can use direct queries for transparent tables. For other business data, you have to leverage BAPIs, which can be automated using the N2One Bits solution.

In essence, you dynamically create your company-specific BI model. The BI model even allows you to integrate external applications using BAPIs, which means that your SAP ECC system gains flexibility and usability without the need for any other software.

4.7 Summary and next steps

In this chapter, I reviewed the techniques and tools you find within SAP ECC for query design. I utilized SQVI and related transaction codes to design a business query. In addition to the already described methods to analyze SAP transaction code use, I also discussed the SQL trace method to identify tables and columns used internally by SAP during the execution of transactions.

Finally, I briefly explored an alternative tool, N2ONE Bits for SAP ECC, which makes the overall query design easier and more efficient to manage.

In the next chapter, I will expand on these concepts and will then define the dynamic SAP ECC Data Model for your specific ECC configuration. In fact, you already have the tools and the knowledge at this point to identify how this may work. You can review your own system to see how to create your dynamic data model.

5 InfoSets in BI Edge 4.1

"Great minds think alike!" is a famous quote that is meant to be inspiring. It means that great minds think alike in the way they think differently from others. Therefore, what it really means is that "Great minds think differently! And inspire new thoughts."

So far, you may have realized that we are not following the mainstream SAP marketing books. Regurgitating marketing brochure content that would just follow the current marketing wave to advocate a new product for each and every trendy demand is not the goal of this book. Instead, I want to encourage what the new SAP CEO called the simplification of SAP product line. I agree with this notion and find that the simplest way is when you use the concepts and technology that is already built in with SAP ECC. Therefore, I am not exploring products alone, but I am touching on the concepts used to build products such as BOBJ BW and SAP HANA and using those concepts to design my own reporting framework.

In this book, you are learning some of the core concepts that are used by BOBJ and SAP HANA to integrate with SAP. In particular, this book is discussing the SAP ECC meta database that comes with SAP ECC, used to extract table logic. In this chapter, I will expand on this concept and use it to create our own meta database model. If you combine this with the transaction code analysis, it is possible to achieve a data model that accurately represents your requirements based on actual system usage.

The main question you may ask is "Why would you need BOBJ BW, then?" You may find your own answer. However, there are some important factors to consider. While you can create your own data warehouse database and run reports and analytics, you can indeed benefit from BOBJ BW content. For example, if you have a multinational SAP system rollout and require a full BI infrastructure, the predefined BW content in BOBJ BW can provide guidance and a starting point for a larger corporate reporting strategy.

Nonetheless, you can utilize the concepts introduced in this book to implement a specialized data warehouse without the overhead of the larger content that comes with BOBJ BW. In this sense, you introduce different thoughts and this can serve as an inspiration for your business intelligence.

In this chapter, we will utilize the *InfoSet concept*. This will add another layer to our current set of tools. At this point, you are able to identify tables in SAP and also know how to create InfoSets in SAP ECC. With this concept, you can essentially group your queries into functional groups. The queries are assigned privileges and are hence integrated with the SAP privilege concept.

First, I will discuss how to run InfoSets outside of SAP ECC. For this example, I will utilize Crystal Reports. In Crystal, you can use the InfoSet data source, which will allow you to connect to the InfoSets in SAP. However, the settings must be correct. You will learn how to make sure the InfoSets actually show up in the Crystal Reports data source. I will use a set of screenshots to highlight the areas where you need to focus.

You can create many InfoSets and organize them by functional module area. You will see an example framework in the form of the company repository. I will then use this example to touch on the limitations of this concept. Finally, I will challenge the limitations and identify solutions to overcome them.

5.1   The InfoSet strategy

The InfoSet concept allows you to group queries within SAP ECC, assign a name, and then restrict access by allocating the InfoSet to a user group. The user group is employed to restrict access.

In order to create an InfoSet strategy, I recommend that you carefully plan the structure. In this book, I recommend a dynamic model based on transaction code use. Using this model, the core areas utilized in SAP can be identified. Then, queries can be created and grouped by SAP module.

You can see how to structure this type of model. On the left side, you can see the organizational chart. Here I employ the commonly used organizational information objects that are part of every SAP implementation. Indeed, these information objects are very different from system to system. Of course, there are crucial differences in the way the system is configured and operates.

For example, I have the following information objects:

- ▶ Countries
- ▶ Companies
- ▶ Subsidiaries
- ▶ Address locations
- ▶ Company codes
- ▶ Controlling areas
- ▶ Logistics: Werke and Fertigungshallen (factories and manufacturing sites)
- ▶ Sales and Distribution: sales offices, sales groups, sales district
- ▶ Material master: Material master records and storage locations

Based on the organizational aspects that determine how the system operates, the actual master data collects and manages data to enable the administration of the company processes within this organizational configuration. The master data and transactional data is the basis for reporting. The reporting data uses key figures to measure the business performance.

In order to limit the scope of our reporting, I use the business process consulting based on the transaction code analysis. I identify the scope in which the SAP system is used and identify how the future system utilization can be improved to better use the investment made in SAP ECC (see Figure 5.1).

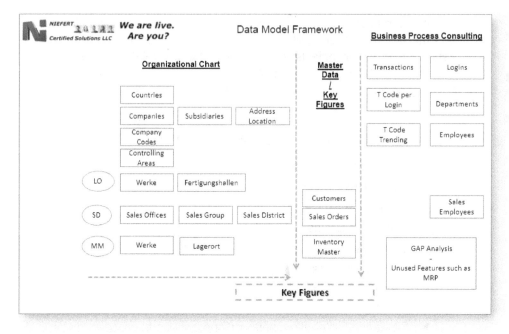

Figure 5.1: SAP data model framework

In summary, I recommend that you use a process-oriented approach to identify your reporting needs and structure them based on the SAP module concept. In conjunction with this, you can use a larger InfoSet concept to cover your reporting needs. In addition, your internal team can collaborate on the model based on its departmental focus.

5.2   Reporting with InfoSets using BI Edge

InfoSets can be used as a data source with SAP BI Edge Crystal Reports. I will look at an example and review how you can make sure the InfoSets show up in Crystal Reports when you connect the InfoSet data source (see Figure 5.2).

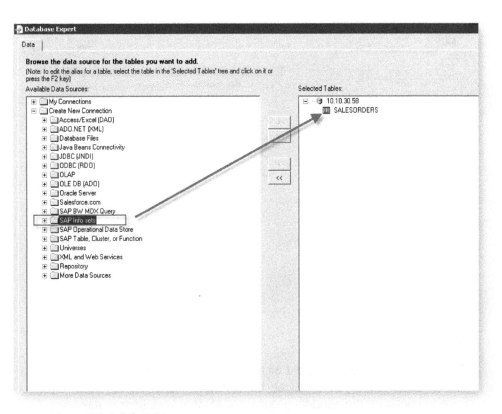

Figure 5.2: InfoSet data source

When you create a new connection in Crystal Reports, you need to choose the SAP INFOSET data source. This will prompt you with the relevant login screen where you will enter the username assigned to you for your reporting project (see Figure 5.3).

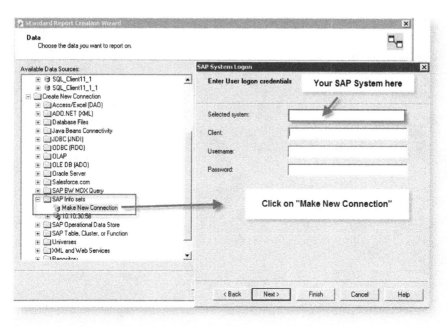

Figure 5.3: InfoSet login

Once you log in, you get a list of InfoSets that can be used as a data source. However, if your required InfoSet does not show up, you may have to configure the security groups in SAP that your user is assigned to. I will review this task in SAP briefly.

5.3 InfoSet and Crystal Reports integration

In the SAP GUI, use transaction codeSQ02 to access the initial InfoSet screen. First, select the name of the InfoSet. In this example, the name of the InfoSet is SALESORDERS. Then, select ROLE/USER GROUP AS-SIGNMENT (see Figure 5.4).

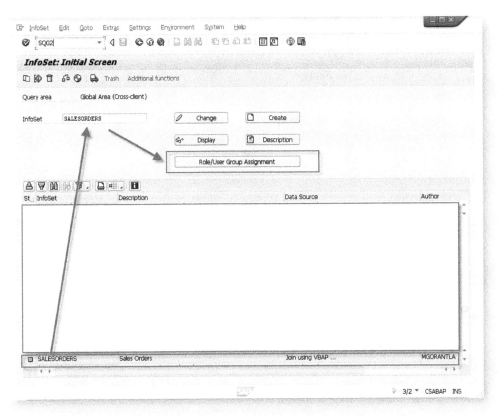

Figure 5.4: Part I—InfoSet role/user group assignment

Once this assignment is complete, make sure that the user group has the relevant user assigned. For this step, use transaction code SQ03, which will take you to the USER GROUPS transaction (see Figure 5.5).

Once these settings are complete, your InfoSet should be available in the Crystal Reports InfoSet data source if you choose the appropriate user.

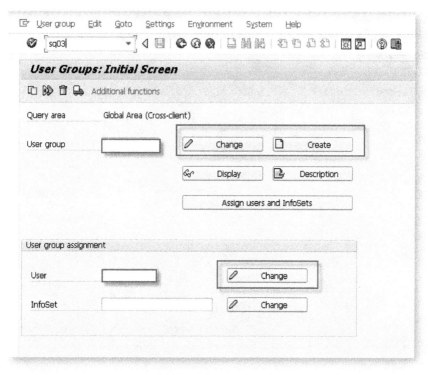

Figure 5.5: Part 2—InfoSet role/user group assignment

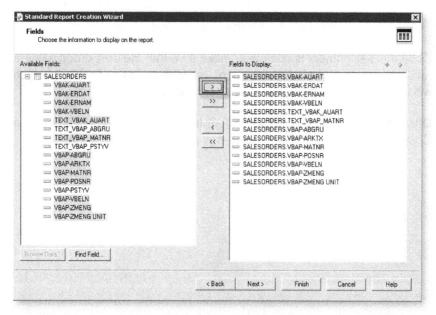

Figure 5.6: Select the fields for Crystal Reports

In Figure 5.6, you can see a set of fields selected for display in the Crystal Report. In summary, you can see that the new InfoSet data source can be used to efficiently report against InfoSets with SAP ECC.

5.4 Create your company repository

As outlined in the beginning of this chapter, I recommend that you carefully plan your InfoSet infrastructure. In order to do so, take a process-oriented approach that has the operational structure of your SAP system as the basis. This will tie your reporting requirements directly to your data. In Figure 5.7, you will see that we move from the business area, which is based on SAP utilization analysis, toward reporting apps and the key figure system.

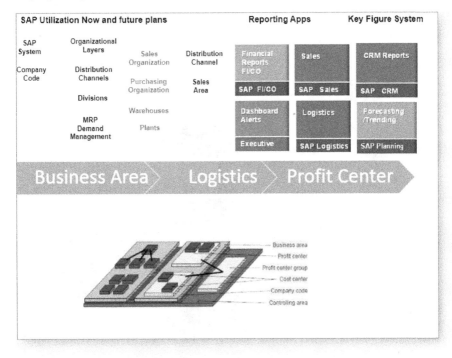

Figure 5.7: From business area to key figure system

The data in SAP is organized in a systematic structure (see Figure 5.7). You can see that the order-to-cash (OTC) process uses a set of documents as part of the overall process. Those documents are structured based on the organizational configuration of the SAP system. Hence, the OTC process includes the following process steps, which collect data via the relevant transaction codes. The transaction codes determine the relevant tables, which reflect the organizational parameters configured for your SAP system.

The OTC process includes:

▶ Sales order (VBAK, VBAP, KNA1, ...)
▶ Picking delivery
▶ Goods issue
▶ Tracking
▶ Delivery
▶ Shipping
▶ Invoice
▶ AR status
▶ Payment

Each process uses backend tables and structures. The information is collected based on the organizational structure, which was configured during the SAP implementation (see Figure 5.8).

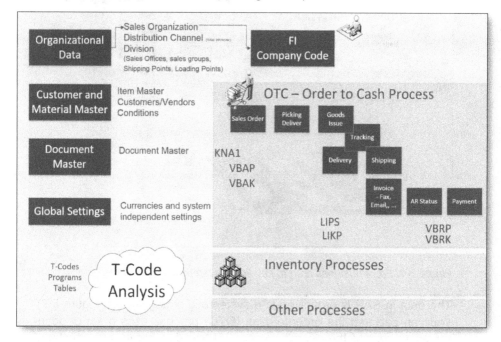

Figure 5.8: Document data and processes

With this concept, you can create your own SAP data model. This can be used to generate reports as well as a custom key figure system.

5.5 InfoSet limitations

While the InfoSet concept is very powerful, it also has some limitations. Those limitations can impact your overall strategy. However, for most limitations, I will recommend adjustments to the concept as a solution.

5.5.1 Only SAP data

The most obvious limitation is that you can only use SAP ECC data within basic InfoSets. If you run reports that require data from other sources, you can extract this data separately and connect the different sources using the universe concept, which I will discuss in the next chapter. In addition, if you need to extract and transform additional data sources, then the data services may be required, which is not included with all editions of the SAP BI Edge suite. I will also discuss the BI Edge versions in the next chapter.

5.5.2 SAP-centric

It is an advantage to use the tools provided by SAP ECC for your reporting strategy. However, sometimes you may not want to further expand on the tools built in with SAP ECC. In that case, you may opt for an external solution such as BI Edge, BI/BW, or SAP HANA. In addition, you can opt for other third party tools and connect the BI elements using the concepts shown.

5.5.3 Performance hit

The InfoSets utilize the SAP ECC database directly. Therefore, extensively using this concept can lead to performance hits, which will decrease the response time of the relevant server. I will show you in the next section how to create your own mini-BI database. Keep in mind that the direct SAP access also has a major advantage—you always have real-time data in your reports.

5.5.4 Not in web applications

There is also another crucial limitation. The InfoSet data source cannot be used if you are planning to deploy your Crystal Reports in an ASP.Net application. Crystal Reports can be embedded within ASP.Net applications. In this setting, you can programmatically pass parameters based on the type of user for example. However, in this scenario the Crystal Reports cannot utilize the InfoSet data source.

5.5.5 Cryptic usage

While there is an advantage to using built-in reporting tools in SAP ECC to create InfoSets, I must mention that the using SAP overall is very alien to non-SAP users. Therefore, this approach can only be leveraged if your organization has a user group that knows how to use the SAP GUI. On the other hand, SAP queries can be used to create an interface for non-SAP experts, who are knowledgeable in basic SQL and BI concepts. They can then leverage the information without having to worry about any specific BI software.

5.6 Overcoming limitations

With every concept, there are advantages and disadvantages. The concept suggested shines here when it comes to creating a lightweight reporting system. However, there are some issues we need to overcome:

- ▶ The query design is complex.
- ▶ Queries can be disorganized without proper planning.
- ▶ The integration of external data sources is not built in with the concept.
- ▶ Direct access to the database may require that we create an additional BI database to prevent performance problems.
- ▶ Traditional queries cannot update data in SAP.

In Chapter 6, I will address each of these issues in depth.

5.7 Company repository download

An essential aspect of this concept is to utilize SAP queries based on system use. The concept addresses the issue that every SAP ECC system has a different configuration resulting in the use of different tables. However, while the tables are different, there is also a common core of tables that are always used. Therefore, I will introduce a collection of queries that are built around the common core. The queries can be used as a starting point to develop your customized set of queries and InfoSets.

I am planning to publish the query sets as open source projects on GitHub. The queries will be organized by functional area. This will be a collection of queries and key figures. The link is not available yet but will be updated on my company website (*www.niefert.com*).

5.8 Summary

In this chapter, we focused on SAP InfoSets. Essentially, InfoSets are the connection to the SAP world. I utilized Crystal Reports to run a report based on the InfoSet data. You learned that there are some crucial steps in regards to the privileges running Crystal Reports with an InfoSet data source. I mentioned that you can create an InfoSet architecture as the basis of your reporting. However, it is vital that you plan properly or risk losing control of the multitude of queries and InfoSets. Finally, I reviewed the possible shortcomings of the concept but also highlighted that these shortcomings can be overcome with proper planning. In addition, you learned about the upcoming GitHub project "SAP Query Bootstrapping." In the next chapter, I will explore a mini-BI system and the common core queries you need to get started.

6 Creating a universe in BI Edge

Up until now, I have focused on the BI tools from a SAP ERP-centric perspective. This was done to help you understand the related transaction codes in SAP that identify tables and transactions, as well as how to create classic InfoSets. Now you can basically run reports without any additional tools, which is a nice skill to have. In my opinion, it is the core skill you need to effectively design BI reporting strategies and also understand the BI tools delivered with SAP as part of the Edge and the BI/BW suite. For example, once you have designed your own queries and start to manage the issues from running reports with millions of rows, you may better appreciate the value you get from the tools that come with SAP BI Edge/BW. However, even with those advanced tools and platforms, you will still benefit from the core skill of running queries against SAP tables directly. As mentioned previously, SAP offers a large set of BI tools, and those tools are rapidly changing and being updated because the BI field is a core business driver. Furthermore, the introduction of SAP HANA as a platform is rapidly improving and will be the core platform for all SAP products in the near future.

Nevertheless, in this chapter, I will focus on the most essential component of BI Edge, the *information design tool (IDT)*. Using this tool, you can design data models and layer the data, which will then be saved as universes. I will cover the core concepts of designing universes and also relate the topic to newer products such as SAP HANA.

I will also clarify that the IDT is of principal importance because this is where data is structured and data sources are connected. It is also here where security is integrated. In order to clarify regarding how to strategize with the IDT, I will further expand on a business model to create a custom mini-BI system.

The mini-BI model will put the universe design process and the relevant tools on a practical platform where you can apply the model design process and structure the tools needed for this process.

6.1   BI Edge versions and patches

When using SAP BI and other software packages, it is extremely important to be aware of the versions and patch levels you are using. Certainly, as this is obvious with all software, you need to understand that, with SAP BI products, it can mean the difference between working and non-working reports. In this book, I used BI Edge versions 4.0 and 4.1 to create the screenshots.

The two main releases for BI Edge in relation to SAP BW that are in production use by companies today are versions 3.x and 4.x. The 3.x versions are fully tested and mature within SAP landscapes. Version 4.x is a major release upgrade with many new upgrades and versions that may require extra work to establish functionality in a complex production environment. For example, you may want to review your specific requirement for data services, which is a separate product and is fully tested with version 3.x. However, with version 4.0, there were initial limitations. With the quick release of version 4.1 though the release 4 has reached a maturity level that can be used in production.

It is important to note that the entire SAP software architecture is going through a major overhaul with the introduction of SAP HANA. Whereas SAP HANA is technically an in-memory database, it is important to note that the impact of this technology more or less touches all SAP products including SAP Business Suite, SAP BW, and all BI client tools. In addition, SAP HANA is the core technology for all cloud-related technologies. In essence, all SAP products will be related to SAP HANA at some point as a main driver. You may want to consider this when choosing BI-related technologies.

Therefore, instead of providing a list of versions that may be quickly obsolete, I would like to further clarify the main strategic product direction, which is relevant for the BI suite. With respect to the above-mentioned SAP HANA platform, there are many considerations.

6.2 Universe versions

The core component of each BI project is the connection and structure of the underlying data sources. In SAP BI Edge, this is done via the *universes*. In essence, a universe structures the data connection from a pure connection perspective toward a higher level that can be used by business users within BI client applications. I will go through an example later in this chapter. With reference to versions, it is important to note that, in version 4.x, BI Edge introduced the *Information Design Tool (IDT)*. It allows you to create a universe and save it either locally or on a BI Edge Server. The IDT is a new tool that came with version 4.x. It saves the universe with the .unx suffix. It is not compatible with the older universe format that had the suffix .unv (see Figure 6.1). Consequently, when you come across the relevant tools, please make sure that you use the newer IDT tool.

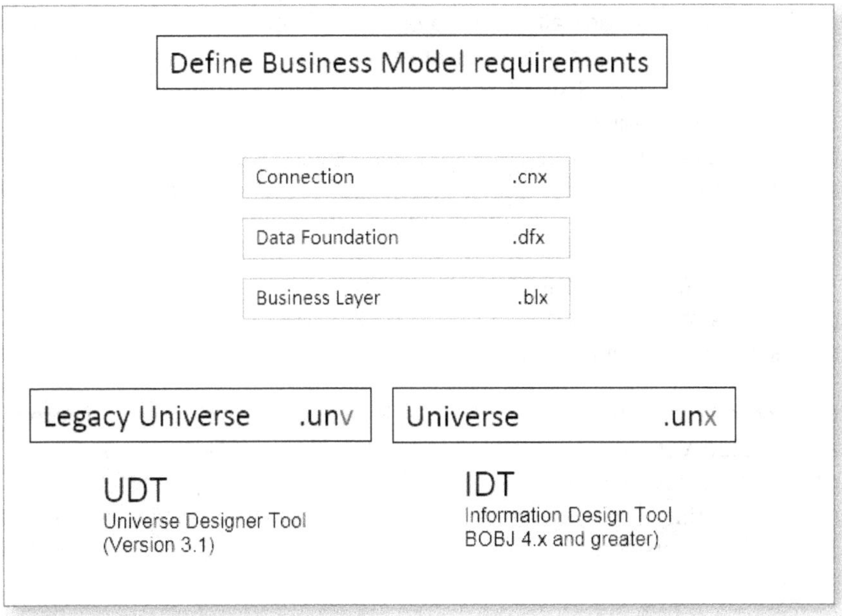

Figure 6.1: Universe versions

6.3   Crystal reports versions

The most common tool for designing reports is Crystal Reports. Crystal Reports has various versions, and it is critical to clarify the relevant product versions so that you can identify the best fit for your project.

The classic Crystal Reports tool is Crystal Reports 2013, which is the legacy upgrade from version CR2008. This version is intended for all customers that have an existing investment with any Crystal Reports-related technology, such as vast amounts of existing reports or embedded reports with Crystal APIs. This version is designed to use the classic universe version from the universe design tool. It is critical to note that the newer universe version is not specifically supported by Crystal Reports 2013.

The other Crystal Reports version is called Crystal Reports Enterprise Edition. Here is where all the innovation and upgrades will take place. This version is designed for enterprise-level integrations within the SAP landscape, including SAP ERP tables, SAP HANA, BW integration, etc. With regards to universe versions, the newer .unx format is supported. However, it is important to note that this new Crystal Enterprise version also supports direct table access against SAP ERP without having to use a universe.

The Central Management Console allows you to configure the relevant parameters for all versions, as it is the Central Management Console to manage the relevant repositories.

One more comment about SAP HANA is needed in this context. There is a dedicated version of Crystal Report with SAP HANA access. This is designed to complement the traditional Crystal Reports 2013 version (see Figure 6.2). It is a separate version and requires that you implement a Linux-based reports server to interact with the backend SAP HANA system.

Now you should have a basic understanding of the relevant versions you may want to consider. In the next section, I will review the modeling aspect and dive into some practical model design strategies.

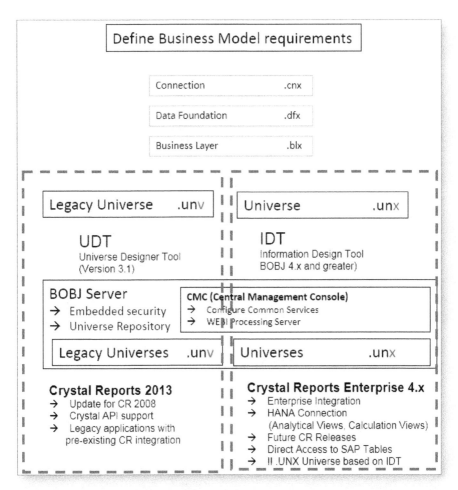

Figure 6.2: Crystal Reports versions

6.4 Repository and KPIs

With the previous information provided about versions, you may start to get an idea regarding the types of problems that are possible during complex BI projects. What if the model design is suddenly running on an obsolete platform? What if the data models and KPIs need to span a strategic timeframe and need to evolve as a collaborative work? In order to address these concerns, it is best practice to implement a KPI and modeling architecture that is not as focused on the tools used but rather on the KPIs and models itself. In order to achieve this, you can manage the models in an independent platform agnostic framework that is not tied to a single version or platform. In this example, I will use BITS to create this meta model (see Figure 6.3).

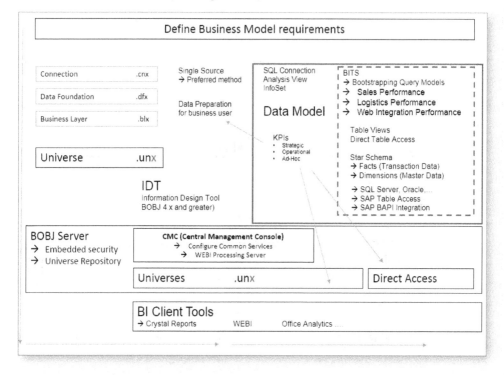

Figure 6.3: Data model considerations

6.5   The present state of BI technology – A critical perspective

In this section, I would like to comment on the SAP overall product portfolio as it relates to BI. A key problem with SAP products in the past has been the notorious complexity of the SAP Business Suite and related technologies. Users often complain that the products are counterintuitive and require technical training to be usable. I mentioned the shadow theme earlier in this book to showcase the hidden problems that live under the surface but are nevertheless obvious to the informed consultant.

When I review the current state of BI as it relates to the SAP landscape, I see a similar trend. In the previous chapters, you learned that many query-related tools in SAP are already built in to the core system. Due to the vast amount of data and previous industry trends, SAP BW was established. It contains BW-specific lifecycle management services and requires that data be loaded overnight in order to be consumed by reporting applications. The BW concept from SAP largely relied on InfoSets. The InfoSets are designed to address the needs of analytical star schemas. BW also provided an easier way view to the master data and transactional data in SAP without the need to understand the underlying table relations, which are highly complex.

However, for the average power user, these concepts often lead to frustration. Instead of getting them to the data, it required that a new BW landscape be implemented. Furthermore, the architecture and thought concepts built into these solutions required a vast infrastructure.

It is interesting to note that, with the latest BW releases, it is still required to use ABAP in certain scenarios to simply join tables. In addition, it is only possible with the newest releases of BW to actually use common SQL tools for reporting.

However, in order to get there, you need to join the huge BW transition towards SAP HANA. This transition simplifies the complex data loading concepts and takes advantage of the extremely fast performance of SAP HANA while keeping proven BW concepts in place. While this transition is working towards a simpler BW concept, it must be said that it sometimes appears complex for no reason. For example, the new composite provider object allows users to connect to SAP HANA, which in return is connected to a BW system, which generates the required schema in SAP HANA, which is driven by BW based on the proven normalized SAP data models. It is a simple concept, but it gets complicated when you do so much to keep the traditional BW alive.

If you followed the concept in this book about transaction code analysis and the automatic generation of table schemas, you may understand how this may be handled in your own project.

In the future, BI architectures should be designed to address the needs of the organization and only then use the technology to leverage the concepts. For example, consider the following criteria:

▶ The data model is a company asset and should be designed to achieve the target industry KPIs and custom KPIs to measure business performance.

▶ The data load processes should be minimized because, with more and more data being produced, it is not reliable to load data into a BW system for analytics.

- ▶ Smart data streams should provide meta information about the data. This would allow BW systems to use analytics that are built into the data stream prior to loading the data.
- ▶ Intelligent data models should consider the way the data is being used. For example, build a version into the data model as well as information about the target systems that can consume the data presented by the data model.

Let's now take a closer look at the current SAP BI architecture as it relates to BW and SAP HANA. You can use this information to design your own models. The core question you may have is: How do I get the data from SAP, BW, or SAP HANA within the current concepts provided by SAP? See Figure 6.4 for an example.

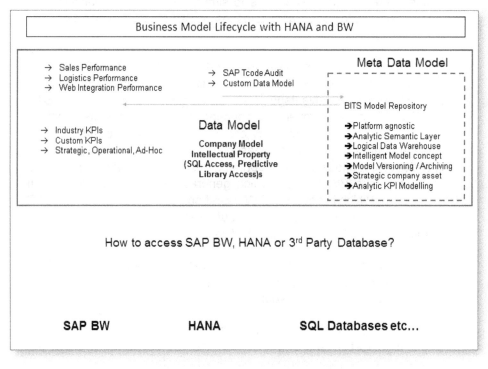

Figure 6.4: Business model lifecycle with SAP HANA and BW

In Chapter 7, I will review the details based on the current release level of SAP BI BW and SAP HANA.

6.6   Connecting to BW, SAP HANA, and others

When you design reports and data models in the context of SAP, you may have to consider SAP BW and SAP HANA. However, these technologies are complex, and SAP HANA is being updated constantly. Therefore, I will provide a current status update about how these products work together in a fully implemented SAP landscape where you find SAP ERP with BW and SAP HANA.

There are many new objects in BW and SAP HANA. However, I would like to focus on the core objects that are relevant to understanding the essentials.

With the new BW release BW 7.4 SP8, you get the *composite provider*. This object will supersede the previously used InfoSet and MultiProvider in BW. The composite provider allows for an inner join or left outer join against InfoSets. In BW, the DataStore Object generates SAP HANA views. Essentially, the data in BW is now transformed into SAP HANA to take advantage of the built-in performance and analytics libraries that come with SAP HANA. This means that you can run queries against millions of rows and get your data almost instantly. If you have ever created a query against a table with millions of rows, you know that performance is a key success factor in BI.

From an architecture perspective, the way the query is running on the lower SAP HANA or BW level is managed by the BW Analytic Manager. The *BW Analytic Manager* orchestrates and prioritizes the order of SQL execution down to the data level. For example, if you have multiple KPIs and they must be executed in a particular order to address dependencies, Analytic Manager handles this automatically. See Figure 6.5.

In summary, if you want to add your own queries, you may want to use the composite provider object from now on.

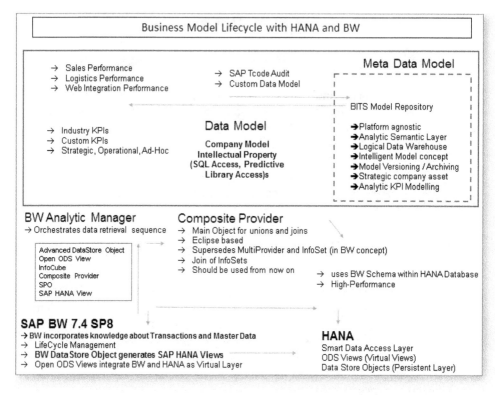

Figure 6.5: SAP HANA and BW integration and composite provider

6.7 Creating your first universe

The universe should be designed with the new information design tool (IDT). You can use the cheat sheet in the IDT to guide you through the steps to create a universe (see Figure 6.6).

The goal of the universe is ultimately to shield the query and data collection complexity from the user who will use the data within an analytics application. The universe also includes embedded corporate security concepts.

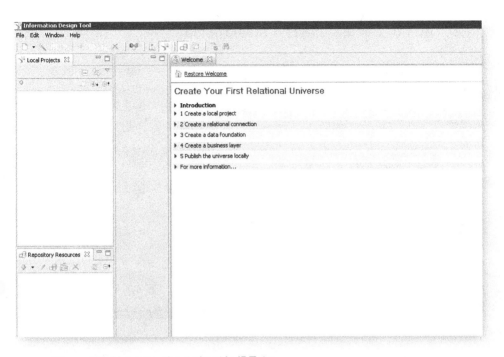

Figure 6.6: Universe cheat sheet in IDT 4.x

Using the steps outlined in the cheat sheet, you can start to create a project and then define the data connection. This will be a connection to a SQL database, BW, or SAP HANA, for example. Following SAP best practices, a single connection concept should be used against a predefined data model. Then, you continue to define the data foundation. This means that you select the tables and columns within your data model to define the data foundation layer. Finally, the business layer takes a subset of the data foundation layer and makes it available for the specific user to prepare a report. Now all of the required layers are implemented, and you can save the information as a universe. The universe can be stored locally or within a BW server where other users can access it if they have the appropriate privileges.

6.8 How to create a universe step-by-step

Following the cheat sheet, I will start to create our first universe with a new project called Espresso Tutorials. All of the relevant layers will be housed in this project. All of the configuration in this project can then be published as a universe.

Next, create a connection. In this example, I will call it SAP ERP CONNEC-TION. See Figure 6.7.

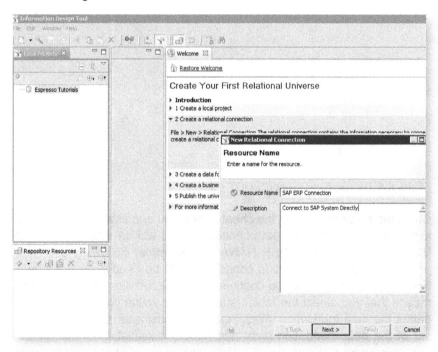

Figure 6.7: Universe create data connection

You will then see a list of the various data connections supported by SAP IDT (see Figure 6.8).

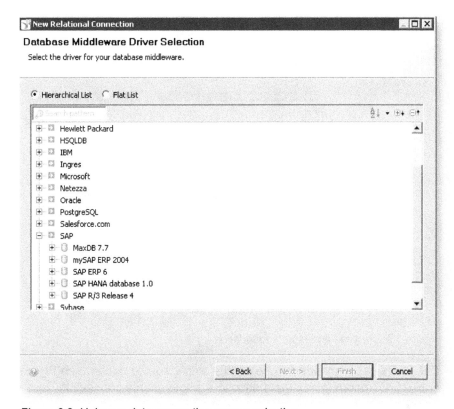

Figure 6.8: Universe data connection source selection

Once I have the essential data connection, I will define the data foundation. The data foundation is based on a data connection. This means I can select the objects I want to use at the data foundation level based on the data connection. In this example, I will use the predefined models in the connection for extracting ecommerce products from SAP All-In-One (see Figure 6.9).

107

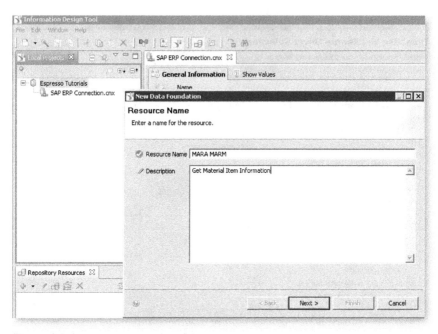

Figure 6.9: Universe create data foundation

Per SAP's recommendation, select the single source option (see Figure 6.10). SAP recommends that I choose a single source connection based on a predefined model.

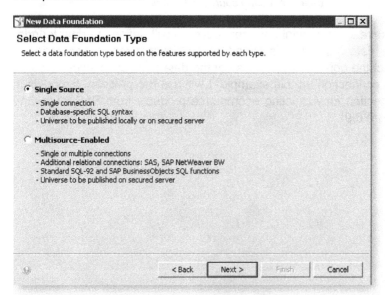

Figure 6.10: Universe new data foundation selection

Choose the relevant tables (views from the predefined model) and save it as the data foundation (see Figure 6.11). I have now successfully established the data hierarchy and can provide selective access for business users to consume data foundations based on their needs. Therefore, instead of offering the full data connection, I am offering a predefined data foundation with preselected tables, views, etc. for the business user. This makes it easier to work with complex data because the business user can focus on the current task versus having to browse through the complete data available in the data connection. This also provides the essential foundation for security concepts.

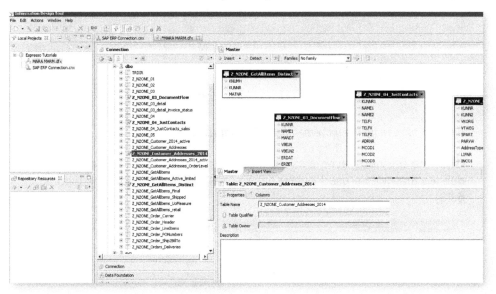

Figure 6.11: Universe data foundation elements

Finally, I created the business layer on top of the data foundation (see Figure 6.12). The business layer is the level of access that the business user will have. For example, a business user can utilize SAP Lumira or Crystal Reports. Based on the connection credentials, the user would have access to the business layer to consume the data within the security context of his or her profile. The business layer can be based on a relational data foundation, which is the case in this example, or it can be based on an OLAP connection.

Figure 6.12: Create the universe business layer (step 1)

Once the business layer is saved, I can assign specific properties to the queries that will be used to present the business layer data (see Figure 6.13).

Figure 6.13: Create the universe business layer (step 2)

I would like to point out a critical setting. It is called the ALLOW QUERY STRIPPING checkbox (see Figure 6.14). If you have complex queries, it may be that you do not need to run all the subqueries to present the result. For example, if you are using certain grouping levels, you do not need to run all the queries to get the details.

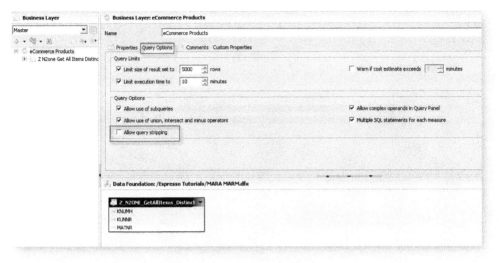

Figure 6.14: Universe business layer option query stripping

When you select ALLOW QUERY STRIPPING, the system will automatically use only those query elements required to present the result needed for the report design.

Please note that, when you create a universe and utilize the universe in a report, certain services are employed to execute the required processes to present the report. You can configure these processes in the CMC. I will not go into detail on this topic but wanted to mention that these services can be configured with the CMC.

Once you have your universe elements configured, you can create a query and run it to see the result. Create the query by dragging the required columns to the right side as shown in Figure 6.15.

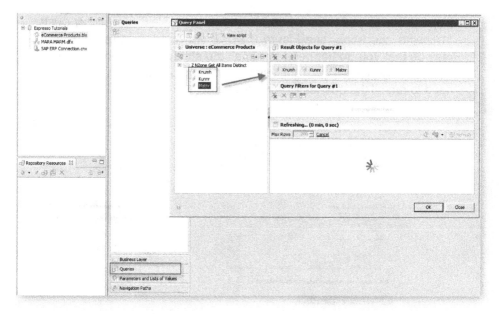

Figure 6.15: Universe query

In the next section, I will review some design principles you can follow to make your universe design project a success.

6.9   Planning your company's universe strategy

Designing a customized universe strategy can be complex. However, it is only complex if you do not plan properly. I may add that a model is more useful if it is simple enough to be understood by the core users, and it can only be expanded and improved if it is in a solid simple state. In other words, if your model is complex, you need to simplify it. The hierarchical concept of the universe design process can help you with that. When you create a plan for your BI reporting project, you may take a step back and define the requirements and goals independent of the tools you are planning to deploy. As you can see with the SAP BI tool, there are many changes and updates. Your BI strategy and models, though, are of strategic importance to the extent that you can look at them as a key company asset. Therefore, you may consider modeling your required data models using standardized techniques prior to creating your first universe.

If you have SAP BW in your IT landscape, you can leverage existing objects based on master and transactional data. However, especially in this context, it is key that you do not get confused by the concepts offered by SAP BW but rather establish your own data model and goals for KPIs.

When modeling the data, it is a good idea to integrate metadata into the model design. Therefore, instead of just modeling the plain data, you can add information and version information about the data you will retrieve. This can then be used to build a hierarchy of models that exchange meta information.

This concept will be further explained on the GitHub site (*www.niefert.com*) where the core set of SAP queries are collected for transaction and master data management.

With this concept in mind, you can then follow SAP best practices in order to best use the available tools.

I will now summarize your project checklist.

Strategic reporting guidelines

- ▶ Design independent of the modeling tool.
- ▶ Design with an intelligent data model in mind.

Best practices for universe design

- ▶ Single source.
- ▶ Query stripping.
- ▶ Use the composite provider for new connections.
- ▶ Understand the architecture from model to connection and database (SAP ERP, BW, SAP HANA, etc.).

In the next section, I will provide further information about the upcoming SAP Data Model Project available in GitHub.

6.10   SAP tables and data model repository on GitHub

When you create queries against the SAP ERP system, you can use a combination of transaction code analysis and related tools to identify tables and ultimately create your own query collection. During many years of work with SAP systems, I have defined a core collection of table descriptions and queries that you can use as a starting point. Those queries are published and updated in a GitHub repository. The link to this repository is available for all readers of this book upon request during the first publication phase.

Figure 6.16 shows the initial concept of the SAP GitHub query repository. It started as a collection of tables in Excel and evolved into a set of essential queries.

In combination with BITS, I created an SAP query model collection that will be hosted on the GitHub repository. The GitHub project information will be updated on the website *www.niefert.com*.

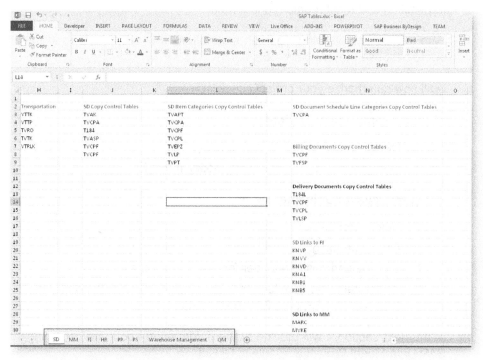

Figure 6.16: SAP table documentation

6.11 Summary and next steps

In this chapter, I reviewed the importance of BI product versions. You learned about the IDT version for universe design. In addition, you should now understand the different roadmaps and versions of Crystal Reports and Crystal Reports Enterprise.

I also discussed the strategic importance of modeling as a tool-independent task. However, a reporting project is always embedded within a specific BI infrastructure. Therefore, we took a closer look at the latest integration scenarios for BI with BW and SAP HANA so that you understand the importance of the composite provider. You can therefore use the right tools when you run a new BI project.

Finally, you learned about the new SAP GitHub project with information about queries and tables in SAP. This will allow you to bootstrap your query projects efficiently.

7 Publishing reports and dashboards

We have reached the final chapter of this book. During the course of the book, a technological and conceptual platform for reporting in an SAP environment has been built. I tried to keep the business user in mind, the one who just needs to get a report done. It is a traditional problem in SAP that you need a team of experts to perform even simple tasks. Today the challenge persists because it is a matter of fact that you often find yourself needing a quick report that has not yet been created in the SAP BW infrastructure. In the beginning, I focused on the existing tools built in to SAP R/3. I also reviewed the technical background to access tables directly. With these tools, you can complete many reporting tasks.

In this final chapter, I would like to conclude based on the information provided that there is a middle ground. The educated user could leverage the SAP reporting infrastructure if it exists but can also ramp up a quick report. Interestingly, this is in line with the latest SAP BI/BW features. These features are focused on agile capabilities, which means the business user can leverage table and report knowledge within a SAP BI/BW landscape.

The takeaway from this chapter will be a clear understanding of the reasons why the SAP architecture appears to be rather complex. As it turns out, there is a reason for the tyranny of complexity imposed on users by SAP. In simple terms, when you report on millions of data records across different geographic regions, things are different compared to ad hoc queries and require a hierarchical solution architecture like SAP BW and SAP HANA. This architecture allows for integrated delta management of data, integrated security with selective access, and embedded BW services. In essence, those topics are all key factors for modern dashboards.

Refocusing all those aspects to the core topic of dashboards, in this chapter I will establish the state of "BI Dashboards." This will be achieved by clarifying the evolution from static graphic-oriented dashboards to the BI Application. I will define the core characteristics of modern dashboards. In order to understand how to connect this knowledge with the SAP BI and BW platform, I will look once again at the smallest unit of reporting in SAP BI/BW. I will review the latest updates available for SAP BI/BW as they relate to agile reporting and dashboard design. Therefore, instead of designing a demo dashboard, I will assess what is "under the hood" of a successful dashboard, the smallest units that allow you to drill down to a detailed level when a graphical representation triggers your interest. You will then be able to design a strategic dashboard platform, one that can sustain modern requirements from visual analysis to drill down with detailed information down to the smallest unit of information.

7.1   SAP dashboard evolution

The demand for dashboards is increasing. The SAP portfolio includes various products that can address this market need. I will briefly review the most prominent candidates and will point you in the direction I believe makes the most sense to utilize for your custom dashboard projects.

The top candidate for dashboards used to be Xcelsius. This tool allowed users to work with an Excel-type sheet to organize data and then publish it in a Flash format. This had pros and cons. On the pro side, it allowed you to create flashy graphs, but with limited backend data integration. Xcelsius also allowed you to utilize web services as a data source to drive the graphs. This was a nice architecture because your data design was driven in the right direction. This is true because, as you will see, publishing data in a web service format is still the method that I recommend for your dashboard design. However, Xcelsius had many limitations due to Flash. In fact, while Flash is available on many platforms, it is not very well-accepted as a business technology.

The current evolution of visual representations in the form of graphics for a dashboard is called Lumira. This solution fully supports HTML5 and related technologies such as JavaScript. In addition, Lumira has some key design elements that make it a preferred application for your dashboard projects.

First, Lumira is highly integrated with SAP HANA. This allows you to not only create dashboards that perform extremely fast but also enables you to drill down to data with a high level of performance.

Second, Lumira has a built-in SDK that allows you to add your own graphical representations using the D3 graphics library. For this, you can use the Vizpackerr tool, which allows you to package your integration for Lumira.

Furthermore, you can use JavaScript and CSS style sheets to format your Lumira applications to your preferred style.

Lumira is available as a standalone application or as a server edition. Then, you also can use the preconfigured Lumira cloud. As you will see in this chapter, the true value of a dashboard is the tight integration with the backend data. This means that all the participating layers of data processing and formatting have to be integrated properly. Since Lumira and SAP HANA are two applications that are very rapid updated and patched, it may be worth your while to choose the cloud-based offerings. This way you do not have to worry about version difference.

Finally, you may want to review a product called Design Studio. This may very well be the central application for business users to design reports with dashboard character. For example, you can copy a Lumira graphic into Design Studio using smart copy and paste. The pasted object will maintain its ability to be edited.

With this quick product overview for dashboards, I would like to end this section and will only summarize as follows: use Lumira alongside Design Studio and design your data based on web services. If you have a SAP backend, then leverage the SAP HANA integration options. This is a brief recommendation, which I think makes sense at this point.

7.2 Key aspects of a successful reporting and dashboard strategy

One important thing to keep in mind as a consultant is that you should not get carried away with new products and technologies. It is of prime importance to keep the user in mind. When you design a solution, you must consider the specific user environment and business role that the potential dashboard user faces.

The user needs to get the results quickly and easily within the current work environment. In addition, the user will not like constraints. For example, if the user commonly works in Excel, then the dashboard may require Excel integration.

In order to achieve this, you may want to schedule user testing with feedback during the early phases of the dashboard design.

The modern user expects to use a dashboard like an application. For example, when a graph triggers a spike, the user wants to drill down to see the detailed data that caused the spike. This allows the user to find relevant data for their purposes. This may very well be the core feature you are looking for. Data and graphics must be relevant. The new paradigm of analysis applications integrates the core features mentioned above for dashboards. In summary, consider the following key aspects during dashboard design:

▶ Design for the user not based on technologies.
▶ Use technologies only to leverage the user requirements.
▶ Present relevant data and graphs.
▶ Integrate with the user workflow.
▶ Allow for data drill down to enable the user to self-service.

7.3   The smallest unit of reporting in SAP BW

Instead of creating a demo dashboard, which you can find elsewhere on the SAP demo and tutorials sites, we can benefit from looking at the other end of dashboards, i.e. the smallest unit of data that drives the graphics. How do you best configure your data backend to work properly for dashboards? Remember that I recommended that you allow for drill-down to enable a modern analytic application. The detailed data is driven by the smallest unit of reporting. This smallest unit of reporting is called the InfoObject in SAP BI and BW terms. If you thought that it was a table column, then read on to understand the difference.

I would say that the InfoObject is the core design parameter that gives the SAP BW reporting architecture its value, but also its burden. For example, when you need to add a simple column to a report, you may wonder why you cannot do that by design in SAP BW. You have to add an InfoObject that will define the parameters for this column. Then, these parameters will drive the way the data in this column is treated within a cube. While this is good, it also creates a lot of overhead. If you want to add 100 columns, then you have to go through a lot of detailed work to make it happen for the InfoObject definitions that are required to accomplish this. Let's look a bit further at what makes up an InfoObject.

In order to define an InfoObject, you review a field and assign it a type with certain properties. The type can be a key figure, for example. The property in this case could be aggregation. InfoObjects add this information to a field (column) and can then be used more intelligently by subsequent data processing layers as compared to a simple column. In a modern BW architecture, the InfoObject would be used in Open ODS views (virtual views) and ADSOs (persistent data representations). Both of these last objects, the Open ODS and the ADSO, are new objects introduced with SAP BW 7.4 SP08. That is why I will review those new architectural changes introduced in BW at this point. Whatever the object used to process the InfoObject, on the top layer, you have your dashboard technology using Lumira, but you also have the BEx queries that will query the data using the additional parameters available in InfoObjects.

Since the InfoObject is a key term, I will define it and provide an explanation.

What is an InfoObject?

The InfoObject is the smallest entity in BW.

How do you define it?

You define the data in an InfoObject by means of types and properties.

What is a type?

Field-level semantics are types. For example, key figures and characteristics. They are used to drill down in reports. Types are also multidimensional semantics and include facts and master data. They are used for aggregation.

How do you use InfoObjects?

You can use non-persistent and persistent representations. An example of non-persistent is ODS views. The ADSO objects are an example of persistent representation.

7.4   The SAP BW platform evolved – AGILE

Traditional SAP BW architecture suffered somewhat from the overhead required to accomplish simple tasks. The new BW version released with 7.4 SP08 introduced some key updates that address the needs of agile users. Most importantly, the issue mentioned in the previous section that required a user to go through heavy overhead to define InfoObjects was improved by giving the user the ability to add external columns to preexisting SAP BW reporting objects. Therefore, there is no longer a need to define InfoObjects. In addition, when defining complex BW models, the user had to define complex star schemas with aggregation tables and dimension tables for InfoCubes. This was required because the architecture was based heavily on extractors that would read the data from the source and would then pre-format the result set into a specific BW database. This required a lengthy procedure. Virtual providers and MultiProviders are examples of this. They can connect to specific data sources and then pre-extract the data to use in BW.

The new objects introduced with BW as of version 7.4 SP08 are simpler and more powerful because they leverage SAP HANA. In this context, it is also important to mention the Open ODS view and the ADSO (Advanced Data Store Object) along with the composite provider. They are the core objects I recommend for your reporting. You may ask, why is this better and more agile than before? The answer is in the SAP HANA architecture and its speed. SAP HANA as a database platform runs the data in memory and, therefore, does not require that vast amounts of data be pre-extracted in tables for later analysis. SAP HANA allows you to present the SAP extractor data in memory and enables the user to combine this data with external tables and columns using the Open ODS view or composite provider. Furthermore, SAP HANA has built-in libraries for analytics and forecasting. Hence, data processing is pushed down to the SAP HANA technical level and enables high-speed performance (see Figure 7.1)

My recommendation for your dashboard reporting project is as follows:

- ▶ Use the latest release 7.4 SP08 for BW.
- ▶ Leverage the Open ODS view and composite provider.
- ▶ Use SAP HANA libraries for analytical data processing like fore-casting and complex analytics.

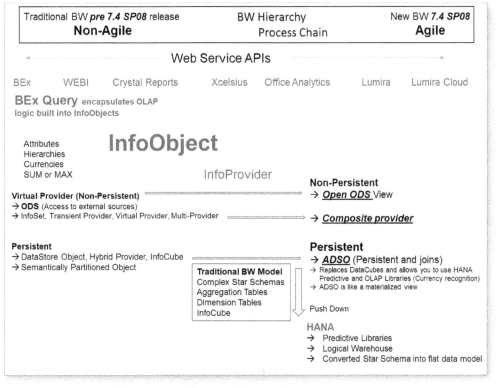

Figure 7.1: SAP BW transition to agile

I have now looked at the InfoObject as the smallest unit of reporting and how they connect with SAP HANA. In the next section, I will review how to best publish data so that it can be used in dashboards.

7.5 Publish the universe for a dashboard

You now understand how the smallest unit of reporting travels via SAP HANA and can be used alongside external tables to enhance your reporting data. The universe can now be published using the Query as a Web Service tool that comes with SAP BI.

When you open the Query as a Web Service tool, you can create a new query and select a universe as a source to generate a web service from the universe (see Figure 7.2).

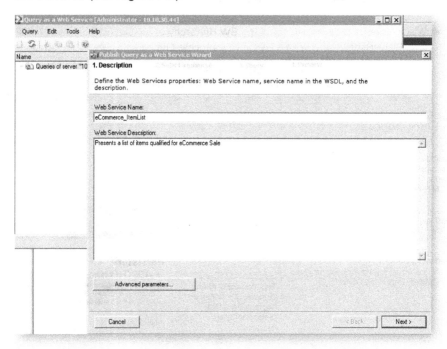

Figure 7.2: Query as a web service

When you follow and click through the wizard (see Figure 7.3), you see that the universe created does not appear on this list. But why? Please note that this exercise is designed to highlight the core architecture of the BI suite, which is BI services and the CMS repository.

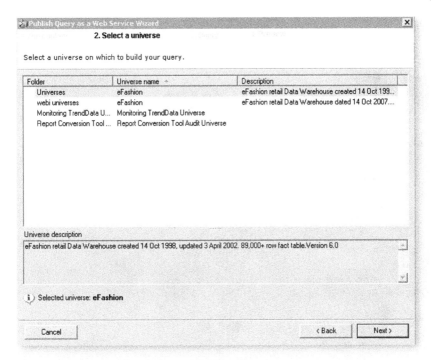

Figure 7.3: Query as a service publishing wizard

I can open the information design tool (see Figure 7.4) and review the universe that I created. It is listed, and I can publish it to the repository. Once the universe is in the repository, I can then hopefully use it in the Query as a Web Service tool if there are not errors. I will show you a common error and how to fix it.

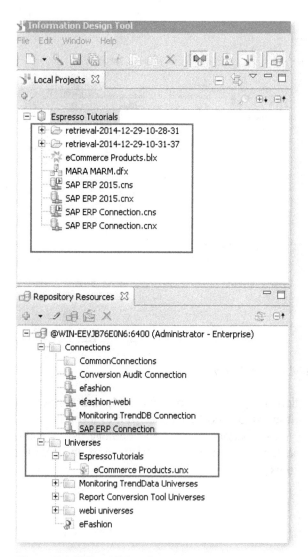

Figure 7.4: IDT publish universe

Select the business layer and then right click to publish it to the repository (see Figure 7.5).

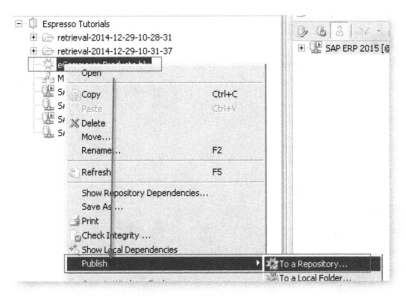

Figure 7.5: IDT publish the business layer

However, when I do this, there is an error message (see Figure 7.6). This error indicates that I cannot just publish the business layer. I need to first publish the data connection and create a shortcut from it.

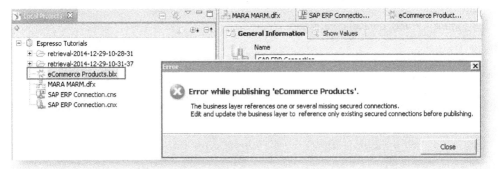

Figure 7.6: IDT publish universe error

Figure 7.7 shows that I publish on the repository server. This is not a local copy, but rather the universe logic is saved within the BI CMS server and can now be used within the BI services. This is precisely the reason why I got the error before. The connection needs to be reformatted when published to work on the server versus just locally on the computer where I designed the connection and universe.

127

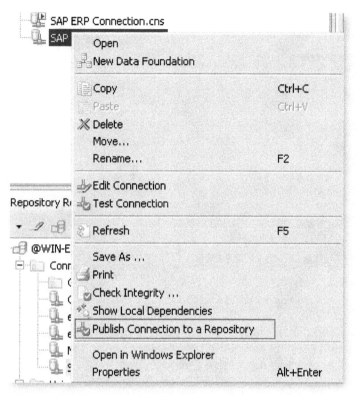

Figure 7.7: IDT publish connection

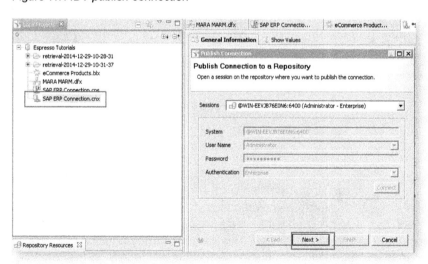

Figure 7.8: IDT publish connection to repository

Finally, Figure 7.8 reveals the last step to publish the connection.

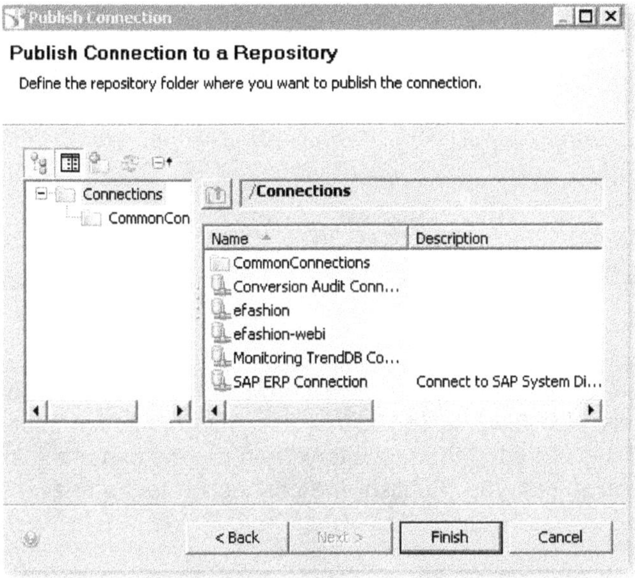

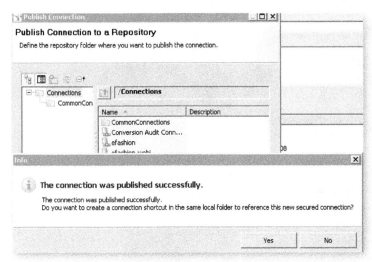

Figure 7.9: IDT publish connection to repository finish

Once the connection is published (see Figure 7.9), I can view it in the repository (see Figure 7.10). However, keep in mind that this was only the connection. I now also need to publish the business layer.

Figure 7.10: IDT publish universe success

Figure 7.11: IDT repository view

Figure 7.11Figure 7.11: IDT repository view shows the repository view with the connections. You have to consider where the connection information is stored. If it is stored in the repository, then reports can use it in the network. It is critical that you "Publish" the connection to the relevant repository.

When you publish the business layer, you have to select the new connection shortcut that the business layer now should be using when it is published (see Figure 7.12).

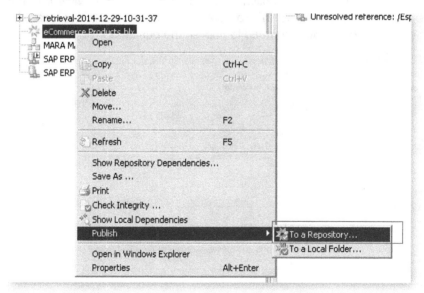

Figure 7.12: IDT publish business layer

Figure 7.12 shows how to adjust the connection for the business layer. You can follow the steps highlighted in Figure 7.13.

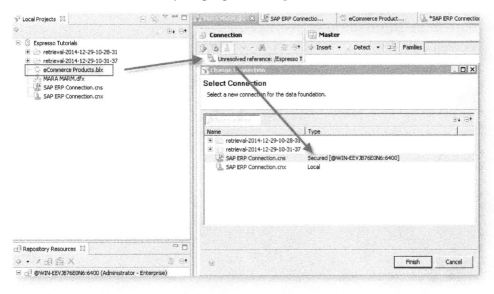

Figure 7.13: IDT adjust the connection for the business layer

Finally, the business layer can be published to the repository (see Figure 7.14).

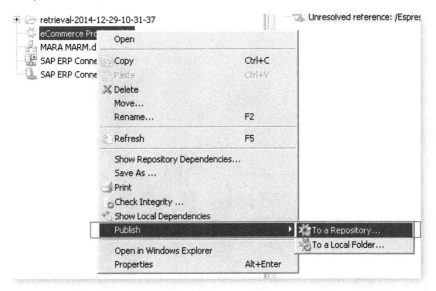

Figure 7.14: IDT publish business layer

Prior to publishing the business layer, you can do an integrity check to ensure that the logic used to query the data is available and can produce a consistent result (see Figure 7.15).

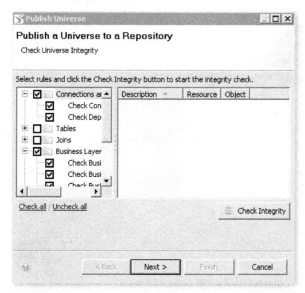

Figure 7.15: IDT universe integrity check

At this point, the universe with the connection and business layer are published to the repository. You can verify this via the IDT by refreshing the repository.

The repository resources in the IDT interface show the published universe (see Figure 7.16).

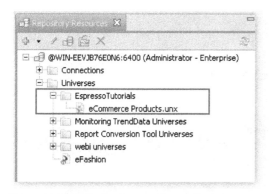

Figure 7.16: IDT check repository with universe

The universe is available in the repository. You can confirm this by logging into the Central Management Console where you can review the universes that are published (see Figure 7.17). You can see the .unx universe. If you remember, the newer universe version is indicated by the .unx suffix. This is the case when you use the new information design tool to design and publish your universe.

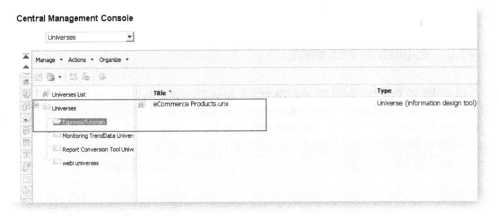

Figure 7.17: Central Management Console showing .unx

When I once again enter the Query as a Web Service tool to check if the universe is now available, I can see that the universe is still not visible (see Figure 7.18). What could be the reason for this?

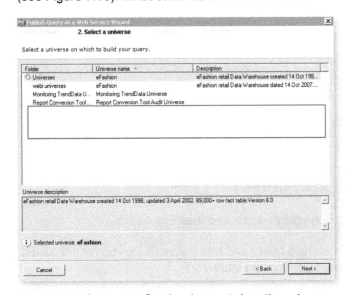

Figure 7.18: Query as a Service does not show the universe

133

This is a good example of the type of issue you can run into when using a solution like SAP BW/BI. There are many tools, and not all support the same level of products. The Query as a Web Service tool does not support the new .unx universes. It only supports the older revision of universes. Does this mean I cannot create a web service from our query? No. I just have to use the right tool, which I will explain in the next section.

7.6   Publish as web service

In order to publish data as a web service, I can use the Web Intelligence Rich Client (WEBI). When you open this application, select UNIVERSE (see Figure 7.19). Now you can see the newly published universe because this application supports the newer .unx universe.

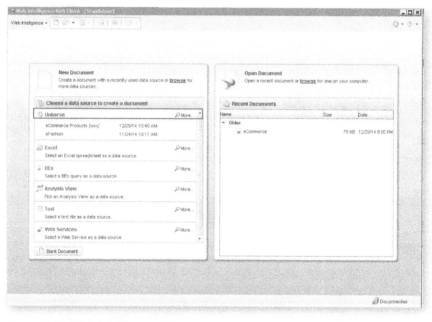

Figure 7.19: Web intelligence rich client

Select the correct universe and proceed (see Figure 7.20).

You can choose a sample query and add the columns you require. Then, click on RUN QUERY as shown in Figure 7.21.

Figure 7.20: WEBI shows .UNX

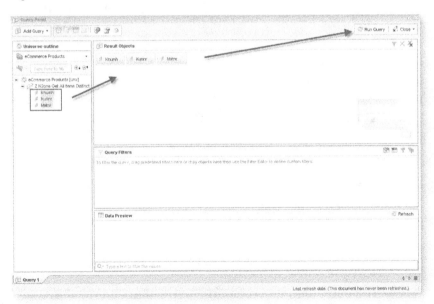

Figure 7.21: WEBI choosing example columns

In the next step, choose WEB SERVICE PUBLISHER in the left section of the interface and connect to the repository server (see Figure 7.22).

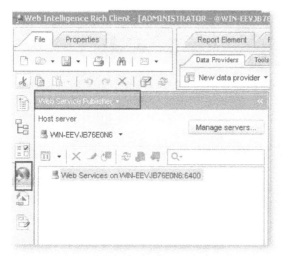

Figure 7.22: WEBI Web Service publisher

Once you see the query result set in the results window, you can select the table that presents the result set. Be sure to select the entire table and then right click to see the menu that has the PUBLISH AS WEB SERVICE button (see Figure 7.23). If it does not show up, then you did not select the full table.

Figure 7.23: Publish as Web Service

If you get an error when you publish, then you have to make sure the right versions are installed for all products involved in this scenario. This includes the repository CMS server, the services, and the WEBI client.

How can you verify the relevant versions? The next section will dive into this topic.

7.7   The BI Edge CMS Repository

The repository for BI Edge is based on SQL Anywhere. Hence, it is not as it was when it was based on SQL Server, but rather in its own SQL server based on SQL Anywhere. The standard installation of BI Edge does not come with any tool to manage this SQL Anywhere server. You can download the SQL Anywhere central management tool (see Figure 7.24Figure 7.24: SQL Anywhere CMS) and connect to the CMS database using the ODBC settings that are implemented as part of the installation for your BI Edge platform.

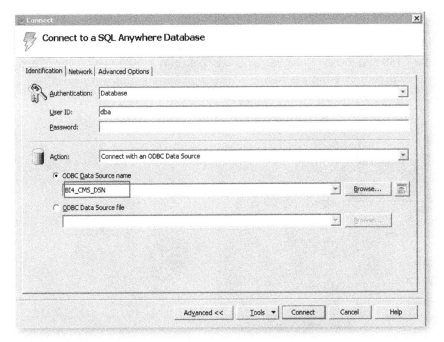

Figure 7.24: SQL Anywhere CMS

You can also use Excel to connect to the CMS and run a simple query to get the version (see Figure 7.25).

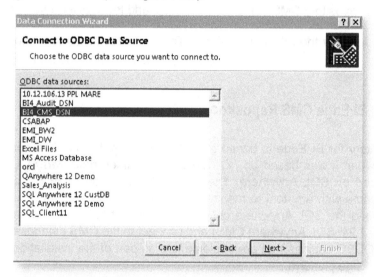

Figure 7.25: SQL Anywhere Repository Query example

You can use the Sybase Central Management tool to visually manage the CMS database. However, you can also run a query using the Transact SQL tool (see Figure 7.26).

Figure 7.26: Sybase Central or SQL Interactive

Figure 7.27 shows an ERD diagram that will help you understand the architecture of the CMS database.

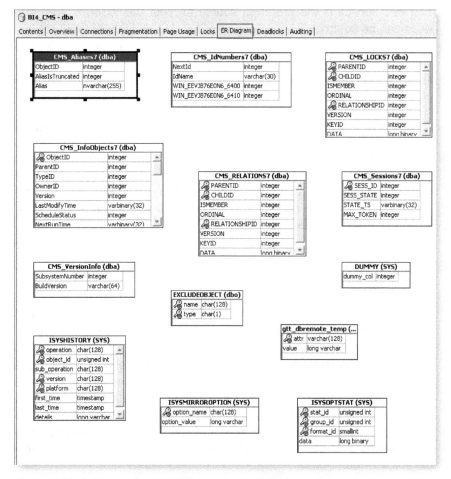

Figure 7.27: SQL Anywhere CMS Repository ERD

The point of showing the SQL Anywhere central interface is to enable you to understand where to look for version information if you have issues with the publication of any of your reports or services. You can also run separate reports against the CMS to get status information about universes and scheduled tasks.

Of course, there is a next step. How can we use the published web services?

7.8 API standards evolving

The web service is the preferred source for your dashboards. Web services can be controlled using APIs provided by the different products that come with SAP BI Edge. For example, the Raylight API allows a user to programmatically control how the BI applications behave. However, using these APIs is not for the business user, but rather for the technical programmer who leverages what the business user can do.

A specific API I would like to mention at this point once again is the Lumira API that allows you to integrate D3 visualizations with Lumira using the Vizpacker tool.

Nevertheless, as you have seen in our example, the business user can easily publish a WEBI report as a web service, which can then be consumed by Lumira, for example.

7.9 Dashboard design considerations

To conclude this chapter and also the book, I would like to reconnect with a theme I presented at the beginning of the book. I highlighted the importance of increasing the user value and usage of BI applications. The newer BI and BW releases of SAP seem to provide the right technologies to achieve an organized workflow for different skill levels involved in a BI project. You may see that this workflow sometimes does not appear to be very simple. However, you may also understand the reason why it is complex. In addition, you are able to add your own queries and columns and can now also connect with BW using the latest technologies available in 7.4 SP08.

I would like to conclude with a list of recommendations for your dashboard design project.

Perfection is the enemy of solutions, and I encourage using custom queries to achieve results quickly. Follow up with new releases to understand what the technology can do, but avoid a religious embrace of technology. Keep you project accountable and focus on the process. However, don't use the process concept as an excuse for complexity. If all else fails, you can use your own ad hoc query using the tools built in to SAP ERP. To get help with that, you can consult the evolving GitHub project with information about queries and reports for SAP. Using these best practices, you can minimize or even eliminate the SAP shadow theme from your project and achieve an improved break-even point for your BI project as shown in Figure 7.28Figure 7.28: BI application break-even.

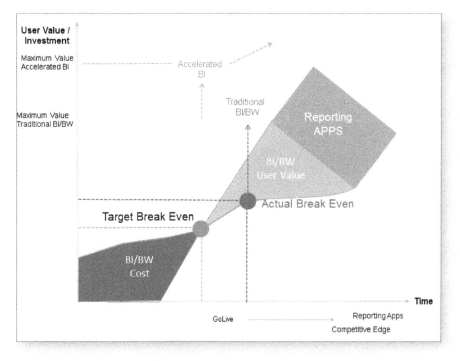

Figure 7.28: BI application break-even

You have finished the book.

Sign up for our newsletter!

Want to learn more about new e-books?

Get exclusive free downloads and SAP tips.

Sign up for our newsletter!

Please visit us at *newsletter.espresso-tutorials.com* to find out more.

A   About the Author

Wolfgang Niefert studied "Wirtschafts-Informatik" at the European Business School in Oestrich Winkel, Germany. The international management program included programs in London and San Diego with a focus on Computer Science and Economics.

He has more than 15 years of experience with international SAP implementations. A certification for SAP Production Planning allows him to relate larger SAP solutions to SAP BusinessOne. Wolfgang also designed the N2ONE Portal for SAP BusinessOne that allows the real-time management of e-commerce functionality.

With more than 10 years of consulting experience in the SAP space, Wolfgang has obtained the SAP PP Production Planning certification from the London SAP Academy.

Wolfgang has worked with HP, Allen Bradley, Sabik, and ATT in Germany, the USA, Saudi Arabia, and Russia.

Expanding your knowledge with new perspective sometimes requires that you evaluate new fields and classic ways of thinking. Wolfgang attended the "Philosophy of Mind" track at Oxford University.

B Index

C Disclaimer

This publication contains references to the products of SAP SE.

SAP, R/3, SAP NetWeaver, Duet, PartnerEdge, ByDesign, SAP BusinessObjects Explorer, StreamWork, and other SAP products and services mentioned herein as well as their respective logos are trademarks or registered trademarks of SAP SE in Germany and other countries.

Business Objects and the Business Objects logo, BusinessObjects, Crystal Reports, Crystal Decisions, Web Intelligence, Xcelsius, and other Business Objects products and services mentioned herein as well as their respective logos are trademarks or registered trademarks of Business Objects Software Ltd. Business Objects is an SAP company.

Sybase and Adaptive Server, iAnywhere, Sybase 365, SQL Anywhere, and other Sybase products and services mentioned herein as well as their respective logos are trademarks or registered trademarks of Sybase, Inc. Sybase is an SAP company.

SAP SE is neither the author nor the publisher of this publication and is not responsible for its content. SAP Group shall not be liable for errors or omissions with respect to the materials. The only warranties for SAP Group products and services are those that are set forth in the express warranty statements accompanying such products and services, if any. Nothing herein should be construed as constituting an additional warranty.

More Espresso Tutorials Books

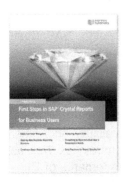

Anurag Barua:

First Steps in SAP® Crystal Reports

- ▶ Basic end-user navigation
- ▶ Creating a basic report from scratch
- ▶ Formatting to meet individual presentation needs

http://5017.espresso-tutorials.com

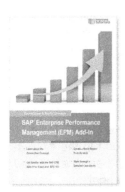

Kermit Bravo & Scott Cairncross:

SAP® Enterprise Performance Management (EPM) Add-In

- ▶ Learn about the Connection Concept
- ▶ Get familiar with the SAP EPM Add-In for Excel and BPC 10.1
- ▶ Create a Basic Report from Scratch
- ▶ Walk through a Detailed Case Study

http://5042.espresso-tutorials.com

Gerardo di Giuseppe:

First Steps in SAP® Business Warehouse (BW)

- ▶ Tips for Loading Data to SAP BW with SAP ETL
- ▶ Using Business Content to Accelerate your BW objects
- ▶ How to Automate ETL Tasks Using Process Chains
- ▶ Leverage BEx Query Designer and BEx Analyzer

http://5088.espresso-tutorials.com

Jörg Böke:

SAP® BI Analysis Office – a Practical Guide

▶ Installation and prerequisites

▶ Analysis Excel Pivot, Ribbon and Context Menu Explained

▶ Enhanced reporting with API and Visual Basic (VBA)

▶ Comparison between Analysis Office AO and BEx

http://5096.espresso-tutorials.com

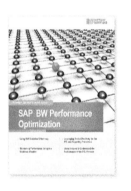

Shreekant Shiralkar & Deepak Sawant:

SAP® BW Performance Optimization

▶ Use BW statistics effectively

▶ Leverage tools for extraction, loading, modeling and reporting

▶ Monitor performance using the Workload Monitor & database statistics

▶ Use indexes to understand key elements of performance

http://5102.espresso-tutorials.com

Rob Frye, Joe Darlak, Dr. Bjarne Berg:

The SAP® BW to HANA Migration Handbook

▶ Proven Techniques for Planning and Executing a Successful Migration

▶ SAP BW on SAP HANA Sizing and Optimization

▶ Building a Solid Migration Business Case

▶ Step-by-Step Runbook for the Migration Process

http://5109.espresso-tutorials.com

Dominique Alfermann, Stefan Hartmann, Benedikt Engel:

SAP® HANA Advanced Modeling

▶ Data modeling guidelines and common test
approaches

▶ Modular solutions to complex requirements

▶ Information view performance optimization

▶ Best practices and recommendations

http://4110.espresso-tutorials.com

www.ingramcontent.com/pod-product-compliance
Lightning Source LLC
Chambersburg PA
CBHW071203050326
40689CB00011B/2231